MAPS

THEIR HISTORY, CHARACTERISTICS AND USES

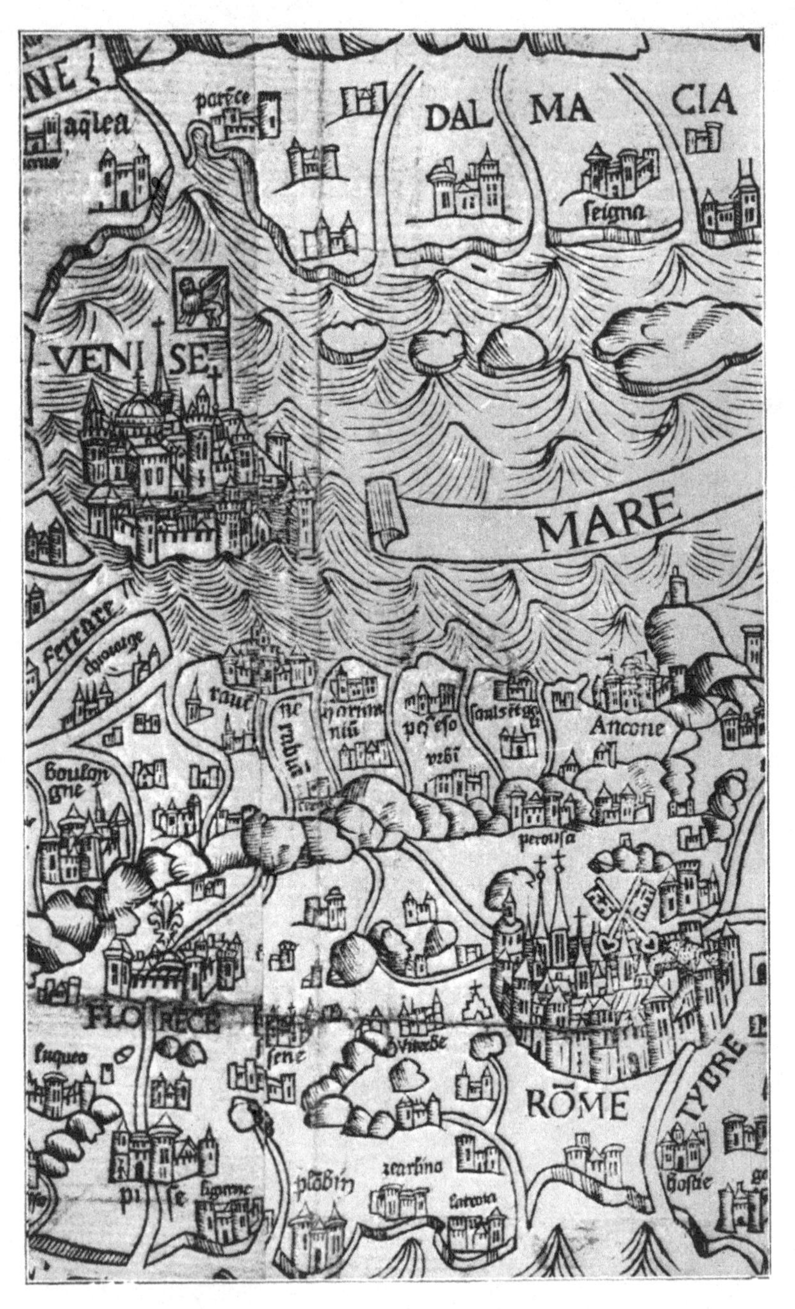

Section from Map of Italy (woodcut). Toussains Denis. Paris, 1515.

MAPS

THEIR HISTORY, CHARACTERISTICS AND USES

A HAND-BOOK FOR TEACHERS

BY

SIR HERBERT GEORGE FORDHAM

FORMERLY CHAIRMAN OF THE CAMBRIDGESHIRE COUNTY COUNCIL AND OF THE COUNTY EDUCATION COMMITTEE

Author of *Hertfordshire Maps: A Descriptive Catalogue of the Maps of the County*, 1579–1900; *The Cartography of the Provinces of France*, 1570–1757; *Studies in Carto-Bibliography; Catalogue des Guides-Routiers et des Itinéraires Français*, 1552–1850; *The Road-Books and Itineraries of Great Britain*, 1570 *to* 1850; *John Cary, Engraver, Map, Chart and Print-Seller and Globe-Maker*, 1754 *to* 1835, and other works

SECOND EDITION

CAMBRIDGE
AT THE UNIVERSITY PRESS
1927

CAMBRIDGE
UNIVERSITY PRESS

University Printing House, Cambridge CB2 8BS, United Kingdom

Cambridge University Press is part of the University of Cambridge.

It furthers the University's mission by disseminating knowledge in the pursuit of education, learning and research at the highest international levels of excellence.

www.cambridge.org
Information on this title: www.cambridge.org/9781107452787

First edition 1921
Second edition 1927
First published 1927
First paperback edition 2014

A catalogue record for this publication is available from the British Library

ISBN 978-1-107-45278-7 Paperback

PREFACE

THIS Hand book is, with but slight alterations, the text of a series of five lectures delivered in Cambridge in the spring and early summer of last year to the Teachers of the County of Cambridge.

The object of the course was that of creating an interest, from the educational point of view, in the rather neglected subject of Cartography, and of supplying, in a succinct and systematic form, materials useful in themselves as suggestions for more detailed study. It embodies the history of map-production from the earliest times, from the point of view of both science and practice and from that equally of the continuous development of the graphic art as applied to the pictorial and technical representation of sections of the earth's surface on paper or other suitable material.

For the Teacher the knowledge of at least an outline of the History of Cartography is essential as a foundation. It alone can enable him to grasp the true elements of the science as applied to the highly conventional map of the scholastic and geographic system of to-day.

It is believed that no Hand-book at present exists which groups in a compact and accessible form the large mass of materials which are actually accumulated in standard works and at our disposal for study.

The present publication is an attempt to supply to the Teacher something in the nature of a Guide, but it is also hoped that it will be considered adequate in itself as an outline and foundation for actual class-teaching.

On the historical side at all events the indications afforded may be sufficient for this purpose.

In the more complex department of art and technique a study of the highest value already exists in the volume: *Maps and Survey*, by Mr Arthur R. Hinks, F.R.S., published in 1913, and which has the advantage of an admirable series of illustrations. To this work reference may be usefully made in amplification of what I have been able to express in my narrow limits of time and space.

In particular I take the liberty of referring the reader to the illustrations published in Mr Hinks's book; for, unfortunately, at the present time the cost of adequate illustration both in number of plates and their technical execution is so heavy that I have been obliged to limit myself here to the reproduction of a few typical and original specimens of early engraved maps, in lieu of the much more extensive series of both ancient and modern maps of which I had hoped to make use.

I may add a word as to my adventure in the original fifth lecture into the field of practical teaching, mainly from the standpoint of Constructive Cartography and of the Elementary School.

It appears to me that teaching from the ordinary flat school map alone is, in the nature of things, essentially dull, and that the imaginative effort of both the teacher and the taught can only be stimulated and a real interest given to geography through a practical application of map-construction to that science, and that as its very foundation.

The suggestions I have ventured to make all tend to this development.

The original Syllabus issued in anticipation of my lectures has been reprinted as, it is hoped, a useful outline of the whole subject, or rather group of subjects with which I deal.

An Index has also been added.

H. G. F.

ODSEY,
March, 1921.

PREFACE TO THE SECOND EDITION

THE exhaustion of the first impression of this little book, the development of the study of cartography generally in schools and especially in the Universities, and the growing public interest in this science, appear to justify a second edition, which is now, therefore, placed at the disposal of teachers and students. A considerable number of corrections have been made in the text. The opportunity may be taken for drawing attention to the second, and revised and enlarged, edition of Mr Hinks's valuable book *Maps and Survey*, which appeared in 1922, and also to a work of great interest, and particularly useful for its profuse illustrations, *Maps and Map-Making*, by Mr E. A. Reeves, map curator and instructor in surveying, Royal Geographical Society, published in 1910.

H. G. F.

ODSEY,
March, 1927

CONTENTS

PART I

SECTION | PAGE
I CARTOGRAPHY: ELEMENTARY IDEAS . . . 1

II THE TECHNICAL BASIS 2

III THE TECHNICAL ELEMENTS OF A MAP . . 5

IV TERMINOLOGY 7

V HISTORICAL CLASSIFICATION 9

VI HISTORY OF MAP PRODUCTION . . . 9
(*a*) Period of Manuscript 9
(*b*) Period of Engraving 13

VII SPECIAL MAPS 19

VIII ART IN CARTOGRAPHY 20

IX HISTORY OF SPECIAL MAPS AND THEIR CLASSIFICATION 29
(*a*) Road-Maps 29
(*b*) War-Maps 30
(*c*) Geological and other Specialized Maps . 33

X PANORAMAS AND THEIR RELATION TO MAPS 34

XI THE ESSENTIAL ELEMENTS OF MAPS . . 36
(*a*) Scales and their History 36
(*b*) Orientation 40
(*c*) Location 42

XII GRAPHIC EXPRESSION OF SURFACE . . 46

PART II

SECTION PAGE

XIII SUMMARY 55

(*a*) History 55

(*b*) Art 58

(*c*) Technical Characteristics 58

PART III

XIV TEACHING: PRACTICAL SUGGESTIONS . 61

APPENDIX 75

INDEX 81

TABLE OF PLATES

PLATE PAGE

I SECTION FROM MAP OF ITALY
(woodcut), illustrating Jacques Signot's *La totale et vraie description de tous les passaiges lieux et destroictz; par lesquelz on peu passer et entrer des Gaules es ytalies*, published by Toussains Denis, Paris, 1515, sm. 4to . . . . . FRONTISPIECE

II MAP OF ANJOU
from *Le Miroir du Monde*, an epitome of Abraham Ortelius' *Theatrum Orbis Terrarum* of 1570, etc., published for Pierre Heyns by Christopher Plantin, Antwerp, 1583, obl. 12mo . . . . . TO FACE 14

III MAP OF HERTFORDSHIRE
engraved by Pieter van den Keere (Petrus Kaerius) in 1599, after Christopher Saxton's map of the County of 1577. From the Latin epitome of Camden's *Britannia*, published by Regnerus Vitellius, Amsterdam, 1617, 12mo . . . . . TO FACE 15

IV TABLE OF DISTANCES FOR HERTFORDSHIRE
measured by the old British mile (compiled by John Norden, and first published in his *Intended Guyde, For English Travailers*, in 1625) with a thumb-nail map of the County. Reproduced from *A Direction for the English Traviller*, London, 1635 and 1636, sm. 4to . . . . . . TO FACE 16

V (A) and (B) PLANS OF FORTRESSES
in France and Flanders, sections from the border, composed of 110 such plans, of the map in the *Atlas Géographique et Militaire de la France*, published by Roch Joseph Julien, Paris, 1751, large 4to . . . . BETWEEN 26 AND 27

PLATE PAGE

VI ROAD-STRIPS
part of the Road from London to Berwick (the Old North Road), from *The Roads through England delineated*, John Senex, London, 1719, obl. 4to. A reduction after the *Britannia* of John Ogilby—the first road-maps of England—London, 1675, fol. BETWEEN 30 AND 31

VII SECTION FROM MAP OF THE AUVERGNE
by Gabriel Symeone, of Florence, illustrating the *Dialogo Pio et Speculativo*, published by Guillaume Rouillé, Lyons, 1560, 4to . . . . . TO FACE 34

VIII MAP OF CAMBRIDGESHIRE
drawn on an initial meridian which should be that of the most easterly of the Azores, making London 24° 30′ E. Reproduced in facsimile from 'The abridgment of Camden's *Britannia*, With the Maps of the severall Shires of England and Wales.' Printed and published by John Bill, London, 1626, obl. 4to TO FACE 44

PART I

I

CARTOGRAPHY: ELEMENTARY IDEAS.

BEFORE dealing with this subject itself in detail, it is desirable to give an elementary notion of the objects of cartography—of map-drawing—and, perhaps, in this connection, it should be made clear that I am here dealing with *geographical* maps alone; thus excluding star-maps, maps of the moon, and possibly some other extensions of cartography beyond the actual surface of the earth on which we dwell.

The natural development of the map is the desire which necessity, or curiosity, imposes on mankind to explore the earth's surface, and to move from one part of that surface to another—working from the known to the unknown—on the path of experience and enquiry.

Thus we have the elements of direction and distance; the main object of cartography being to give graphic expression and permanency to these elements. The result is a map—of course in its most rudimentary form.

What is the first point? It is clearly *direction*, and the savage man who desires to move—prompted by the observations he may have made as to natural phenomena (the flow of water in rivers, the ridges and ranges of mountains within his view), the information he may receive from others as to fertility, or the presence of means of existence at a distance—has first to deal with this problem. His standard of direction is, in the main, the sun in its regular risings and settings, in a less degree may be established by well-recognized stars, and, in detail, is associated with water boundaries, the direction of water flow, and these factors he can communicate by word of mouth or by the drawing of maps.

Distance is a secondary factor in the case. We are none of us competent, in practice, even to-day in our highly civilized state, as individuals, without the aid of instruments of precision, to determine weight and measurement, or to compute time or space. In fact we are singularly deficient in these appreciations. The savage does not measure distance except in terms of time. Even to-day, in mountainous districts, in climbing the cross-country travel, no one thinks in terms of miles or kilomètres. So many hours is the measure. In climbing in the Alps, for instance, one never gets into one's mind any idea of kilometric distance. The guides give the times which a particular journey across the mountains, or a particular ascent, will take according to the circumstances—mainly of the weather.

We come back to this, that a rudimentary map is a route-map, a travel-map, a road-map—in *one* direction—with the gradual development of collateral details.

Similarly, sea-charts were built up in early times by point to point observation of the coast-line, no mariner in those days facing the open sea, without the pressure of great necessity, or except to a very limited extent.

These are the natural and fundamental ideas upon which maps have been built up, and it is well to keep these ideas of origin well and permanently in mind, especially in regard to teaching.

II

THE TECHNICAL BASIS.

The object of the cartographer—the map-maker—is to lay down on a flat surface—in modern times of paper—a pictorial representation of a portion of the earth's surface.

For this purpose it is obvious that certain conventional arrangements must be arrived at. The building up of these conventions has, of course, its own history. Art and convenience have gradually reached what we now universally accept to-day in this respect. While maps are drawn to scale, as regards general dimensions, and the distances between points of importance, the indication of details is universally pictorial. A town is represented by a dot, a road or river by a broad line which is perhaps fifty or a hundred times wider than the object represented, if drawn on the true scale of the map. Variations from a plane surface are similarly treated in a highly technical manner. Elevations and depth in water are represented by forms of shading, or the drawing, upon a system, of horizontal lines, or by colours. In the adaptation of all this method and convention, the objects of the particular map must be, of course, specially considered. The cartographer in most cases aims at giving pictorial value to the dominant features of the district, or country represented, in particular to natural features, such as the flow of water in rivers, coast-lines, the character and altitude of high plateaux and mountain ranges, and to such artificial features as the location of populations and of centres of industry and commerce, the means of travel and communication—which may in some cases mean the map of a road or railway with marginal details—and, finally, to special features, geological features for example and others, possibly, relating to climatic conditions, and questions of population and race, and broad features of marsh land, ice, sandy wastes, and so on. The map-maker must, in all cases, just as the landscape or portrait painter must, settle his mind on the limits and objects of his particular composition before he begins his work.

We may also have special maps, as, for instance, of the

roads, or of the rivers, of a country, of which the French maps of Nicolas Sanson of 1632 and 1641 respectively are good early examples.

A map is pictorial—as it represents a surface as a conventional picture; it is scriptorial—in respect of the written details and explanations. The limits of both must be settled. At one time a number of maps of the English Counties were published, almost covered with descriptive text. An example of this eccentricity is found in the *Atlas Anglicanus*, by Emanuel and Thomas Bowen, published about 1770. The practice has not been followed and is not to be commended. Even the writing of the necessary names on a map is a subject of much art and ingenuity if the pictorial clearness of the map is not to be obscured. The maps of Sanson and of other cartographers of the seventeenth century, and even earlier, are sometimes curious in consequence of the practice adopted of writing the names of countries and provinces in single letters distributed about the map in the places the most free from detail, and in some cases it is quite a hunt to pick up the whole of a title. I may instance a map of the *Isle de France* in the *Cartes Générales de Toutes les Parties du Monde*, Paris, 1658.

To sum up these observations—a map lies in character between a book and a picture, and combines the features of both. The classification and the bibliographical description of maps are thus difficult, and require a good deal of attention[1].

The decorative art in relation to maps was very prominent in the early stages of map-making. It disappeared when the geographical accuracy and scientific representation of surface became the dominant object (as it now is) of the carto-

[1] A discussion of this matter will be found in a paper I communicated to the Bibliographical Society some years back, which is reprinted in my *Studies in Carto-Bibliography*, Oxford, 1914.

grapher. The illuminated maps of the Jaillots of the end of the eighteenth century, and two very beautiful sheets of the neighbourhood of Naples of 1793 and 1794, drawn by Rizzi-Zannoni, are, I believe, the finest specimens extant of this decorative art.

Simplicity is an important object of the cartographer; its combination with graphic detail is an essentially difficult problem; when colour, in outline, or super-imposed over the whole area, is introduced, this problem becomes more difficult still. A critical comparison of the official maps of half-a-dozen European Countries would establish at once to the eye the truth of this observation. Rizzi-Zannoni had an almost marvellous success in treating his map-surface in the most elaborate detail without destroying the pictorial effect of relief and of variety.

Maps are reproduced in various ways, but in general from engraved plates. The questions involved are not discussed here, and it is doubtful whether such a discussion is at all necessary to the completeness of my *exposé*, although, no doubt, it might be made of great artistic and professional interest when fully and adequately treated by experts.

III

THE TECHNICAL ELEMENTS OF A MAP.

To treat now of the technical elements of the map. Of these, three are absolutely essential.

There must be a *scale*. The scale is the measure of proportion between the picture and the area of the earth's surface represented. Without a scale a map is of no practical value; it is a vague sketch and conveys to the reader no concrete impression of size at all.

There must be *orientation*, that is to say there must be some clear indication of direction. The common, and now well-established, practice is to arrange the map with the true north at the top. This is, of course, a purely conventional method, and, as regards plans on a large scale, is not always followed. But any variation from this arrangement is met by drawing on the map an arrow, or other indication of the directon of the points of the compass, so that the map can, if necessary, be placed in its true position relatively to the area it represents.

Location may not be necessary in plans, but it is certainly desirable in anything that can be called a map, and in all maps of large areas it must be regarded as essential. By location I mean indications which enable the reader to place the map correctly on the earth's surface, and relatively to other maps and sheets on the same or different scales.

For map-drawing, as I have already pointed out, technical and conventional methods are essential, and have come now to a stereotyped uniformity. This matter, with the others mentioned above, will be treated more fully later. I may, however, call attention in connection with the study of all these details, to the Army *Manual of Map Reading and Field Sketching*, 1912 (*Reprinted, with Additions*, 1914), which can be purchased for a shilling. It contains a mass of most valuable and suggestive material, admirably arranged, condensed and illustrated, and, although it is drawn up from a purely military point of view, has a general educational value from which every teacher of geography and every student of the practical use of maps can derive assistance. The following opening sentence in this handbook is worth quotation:

An officer, or non-commissioned officer, may be said to be proficient in map reading when on examination a map conveys to him a clear impression of the ground features as represented by contours or shading, and of all the natural or artificial features exhibited on the map. Further, he should be able to identify his position on the ground quickly and to recognize all visible objects marked on the map.

This requires close study and constant practice, and is an important branch of military education.

The view I desire to impress upon teachers with regard to the proper treatment of maps as instruments of knowledge and study is in close harmony with this statement in its general bearings.

IV

TERMINOLOGY.

Before passing from the introductory part of this study it is as well to deal with Terminology, which has both an interest—mainly historical—of its own and an instructional value which should appeal to the teaching profession.

When, in the latter half of the sixteenth century, maps began to accumulate as the result of the general development in copper-plate engraving and printing, no name existed for the books into which they were collected. Ortelius, who published, in 1570, the first systematic collection of maps, which was printed at Antwerp, in the famous printing establishment of Christopher Plantin, gave it the title of *Theatrum* (or a display, or show). This was followed by John Speed in England (*Theatre of the Empire of Great Britaine*), by Maurice Bouguereau, the printer of Tours, in his *Théâtre François*, and by his successors Jean Le Clerc and Jean Boisseau, and also by Melchior Tavernier. In the meantime Gerhard Krämer, who is better known in the latinised form of his surname as *Mercator*, working on parallel lines to those of his friend Ortelius, had built up a collection of maps which, it is said, he withheld from publication in order to assist Ortelius in the sale of his venture. Mercator died before this collection was actually published, but he had chosen for it the symbolical and mythological title of *Atlas*. This is, in itself, a rather far-fetched adaptation of the Greek mythology, in which Atlas was known as the being who supported on his shoulders the pillars on which the sky rested, pillars which were thought to rest in the sea, immediately beyond the most western horizon. But, whatever the idea may have been in the choice of this name for a collection of maps in book form, its shortness seems to have given it favour, and it has survived all its rivals and is now well-established in cartographical nomenclature. Amongst other terms employed in the same sense were *Speculum* (*Speculum Orbis Terrarum*), Gerard de Jode (*c.* 1578), and *Speculum Britanniae*, used by John Norden in 1593; *Geographia*, *Cosmographia*, and *Chorographia*; but none of them had any success. For individual maps, the word *Map* itself came into use in the Middle Ages, the name *Mappamundi*, or *Mappemonde*, being explained as showing that maps were originally painted on cloth. We have restricted the use of this designation to land-maps, having adopted *Chart* for sea-maps, which was, as early as the fourteenth century, used in this sense (*carta nautica*) though it did not come into general use till two centuries later. The word *Type*, from the Greek, is sometimes found. The Romans called a map *Tabula*, and Mercator, in anticipation of his atlas, made use of the same term to describe a set of maps of France, which he issued in 1585 (*Galliae tabule geographicae*). We have beside the name *Portolano*, which was used in the Middle Ages to designate the charts of the Mediterranean. But, out of all this groping for suitable names, with us in England, *Atlas*, *Map* and *Chart* remain in exclusive possession.

V

HISTORICAL CLASSIFICATION.

In the historical classification of maps there is, as in the study of books, the great natural division between the period anterior to the discovery of the art of printing and of impression, and that of easy multiplication of examples by the latter method.

In a broad way the dividing line may be taken at 1500; but the earliest dated printed map is of 1460, and it must be remembered that the *Theatrum* of Ortelius appeared in 1570. This intermediate century may be regarded as a period of transition.

Bearing in mind this division, I go back to the early history of cartography as it is known to us in Europe and the more or less approximate arrears of Asia and Africa.

VI

HISTORY OF MAP PRODUCTION.

(*a*) Period of Manuscript.

Adopting this geographical limitation for the moment, it is amongst the Egyptians that we find the earliest recorded examples of cartographic representation, many of them mural; maps and plans have actually been discovered on old Egyptian papyrus rolls.

To the Babylonians is attributed the high distinction of having originated the division of the ecliptic into twelve signs, and, later, into 360 degrees. The division of the circle into this number of degrees, and the further divisions of 60 minutes and 60 seconds, as well as the corresponding division of the day into 24 hours, were the outcome of their sexagesimal system of numeration.

Adopted by the Greeks, and by Ptolemy, the scientific elements necessary for the astronomical determination of geographical position became available, and cartography at once advanced to the certainty of a science.

It does not fall within the plan of this treatise to review the progress of cartography amongst the Greeks prior to the time of Ptolemy, but it may be well to mention the world-map of Hecataeus of Miletus, of about 500 B.C., and to notice the great advance for which we are indebted to the famous astronomer and geographer, Eratosthenes of Cyrene, the keeper of the Alexandrian library (276–196 B.C.). He recognized the spherical form of the earth, and was the first to make a rational geodetic measurement for the purpose of determining its size. This work is stated to have been approximately correct, but, unfortunately, a later astronomer, Posidonius (about 130–50 B.C.) reviewed the conclusions of Eratosthenes, diminishing his arc of the meridian by one-third, and from this error, adopted by Ptolemy, there resulted an exaggeration of the longer axis of the Mediterranean by a third, and a distortion of all the Mediterranean countries, which, although the error was corrected in the compass-charts of that sea of the Middle Ages, was perpetuated in cartography until as late as 1700.

When Columbus set out to discover—not a *new* world but the eastern shores of the Indies—he seems to have founded on the errors of Ptolemy and his immediate predecessors, which, in effect, ignored the space on the earth's surface occupied by both the American Continent and the Pacific Ocean. Had he accepted the working charts of the Mediterranean drawn by navigators, and from them deduced a reversion to the approximately correct calculations as to the dimensions of the earth of nearly 2000 years earlier, it may well be doubted whether the space to be travelled to reach the land, which would, in the ignorance then existing of the American Continent, have appeared prodigious, must not have daunted the enthusiasm even of Columbus and have postponed his discoveries perhaps for a generation.

Ptolemy (Claudius Ptolemaeus), a native of Egypt, flourished in the second century after Christ. He was famous as an astronomer and a geographer, and his work seems really to have been that of applying the former science to the fixing of the points on the earth's surface necessary for the drawing of maps. He does not appear to have been responsible for map-drawing himself, and his fame, in modern times, is due to the discovery of his *Geographia* in the fifteenth century, from which an edition in print and translated into Latin appeared in 1475. The maps compiled from the data supplied in the *Geographia*, issued in atlas form in a long series of editions, were the foundation of cartography as a modern science. Their errors vitiated the maps of Europe and the adjoining continents for two centuries, but, at last, were dissipated when maps began to be constructed on actual surveys and triangulations.

Before passing on to the period which followed the so-called revival of Ptolemy, it is proper to remind my readers that, in sequence to the Greeks, the Romans were map-makers, but they, as a practical people, seem to have limited their activity in this direction to mere map-drawing for military, topographical, and administrative purposes. They added nothing to exact knowledge of cartography, and, with one exception, nothing of their work has come down to us. That exception is the famous *Tabula Peutingeriana*, now preserved in the National Library at Vienna. It is a curious, distorted and diagrammatic representation of surface, in the nature of a road-map, in twelve sheets, forming one long strip, and has very little real cartographic interest.

Quite collateral to other progress in map construction, the portolan charts of the Mediterranean and the Atlantic coasts of Europe and Africa, ultimately extended to the coast of the Brazils, have a character and importance of their own. By using the mariner's compass, which reached them through the Arabs, the coastal navigators of the Mediterranean—Italian, and Catalan, with but few exceptions—attained, by putting together their observations and charts, painted on skins, to a very accurate delineation of that sea. Of this subject I think the best study is contained in *Portolan Charts, their Origin and Characteristics*, by Dr E. L. Stevenson, published in New York in 1911.

These coast-line charts are drawn in colours, and, being navigators' charts, exhibit no details of the land, though they are frequently ornamented with fanciful designs representing towns and other features adjacent to the shore line. None of those extant is known to be drawn prior to the year 1300, the oldest dated example being that of the year 1311, signed by Pietro Visconte. No doubt earlier charts existed, as it is recorded in a work by Guillaume de Nangis, in describing the crusade of Saint Louis (Louis IX of France), in 1270, that, in the voyage from Aiguesmortes to Cagliari, in Sardinia, the port selected for the rendezvous of the ships making up the expedition, the fleet was overtaken by a storm, and at the end of the sixth day, as Cagliari had not yet been reached, the King expressed a wish to know the exact location of the ship. Thereupon, we are told, the pilots brought to him their charts, and showed him that the port was not far distant.

More than 500 of these manuscript charts are known to exist, distributed through 54 public and private libraries. The British Museum possesses 52. They have a range in time up to the sixteenth century, and the latest examples extend geographically so as to show the whole of the African coast-line and a large section of the Atlantic coast of the American continent. Some interesting technical points connected with these charts will be noticed later; but I cannot leave this subject without calling attention to the Portuguese charts of the early part of the sixteenth century, which bear a close resemblance to the portolan charts in both art and technique. They are more highly decorated than anything I have seen amongst the charts of the European coasts. There is also, in the British Museum, an anonymous Italian map of the coast-lines of South and Central America, of about 1513, which is worth attention.

(*b*) Period of Engraving.

Manuscript maps overlap slightly, in point of time, the new engraved cartography which, from Ortelius to our own times, has flooded the world with its productions. Indeed, the productivity, in the first instance of the Dutch and Flemings, and contemporaneously, and later, of the cartographers of other European nations, is very extraordinary. Even in 1570, Ortelius could count nearly 100 known cartographers, and, in later issues of his *Theatrum*, the list rises successively to 134 and 170 names[1]. The Dutch school was most prolific. Following Ortelius (1527–98) and Mercator (1512–94), the three families of the Hondius, the Blaeus, and the Jansons issued, in commercial rivalry, enormous atlases, some of them running to eleven and twelve tomes, duplicated with the text in most of the European languages. This Dutch school hardly covered a century of time, and seems to have died out rather abruptly. The French school, founded by the famous cartographer, Nicolas Sanson, of

[1] An epitome of the *Theatrum* was issued from the Plantin press, by Philippe Galle, with the title *Le Miroir du Monde*, Antwerp, 1583, etc.

Abbeville, flourished from before the middle of the seventeenth till quite the middle of the eighteenth century, with two of the sons of the original Sanson, Adrien and Guillaume, their collaborators and successors, the Jaillots, and the Robert de Vaugondys, father and son, who published atlases well into the second half of the eighteenth century.

This school—in which the art was largely of Northern France, Picardy in particular—was preceded by a series of national atlases, now of great rarity, of which the first is the *Théâtre François*, published at Tours in 1594, of which very few copies are at present known to exist. The plates for this atlas were copied, most of them, from Ortelius and Mercator, and by a Fleming, Gabriel Tavernier. The contract for this work, in great detail, still exists in the notarial records of Tours. The *Théâtre François* was reprinted, with additional maps, by Jean Le Clerc and by his widow, from 1619 onwards, and later again by Jean Boisseau. Melchior Tavernier, of Paris, who at first published for Sanson, until some disagreement brought the latter to Paris, from Abbeville, to personally supervise the issue of his own maps and atlases, also published an important collection of maps, mostly copied from the Dutch, in 1634. These antecedent efforts in cartography in France have no direct connection with the work of Sanson, except in historical sequence.

But it must not be thought that the British Isles were not represented in early times in cartographic production.

The first engraved map of England and Wales published in this country was the work of a Welshman, Humphrey Lhuyd of Denbighshire, and was published in 1569, but Mercator had, a few years earlier, drawn a large and accurate map of the British Isles, of which the manuscript, dated 1564, has recently been discovered at Breslau. It has never been engraved, but has been reproduced by photography.

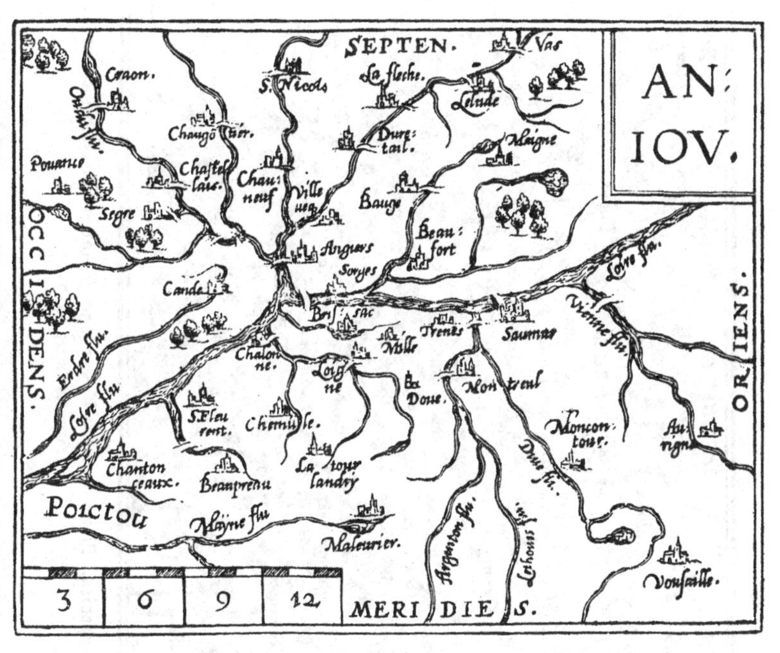

Map of Anjou, from *Le Miroir du Monde.*
Christopher Plantin. Antwerp, 1583.

PLATE III

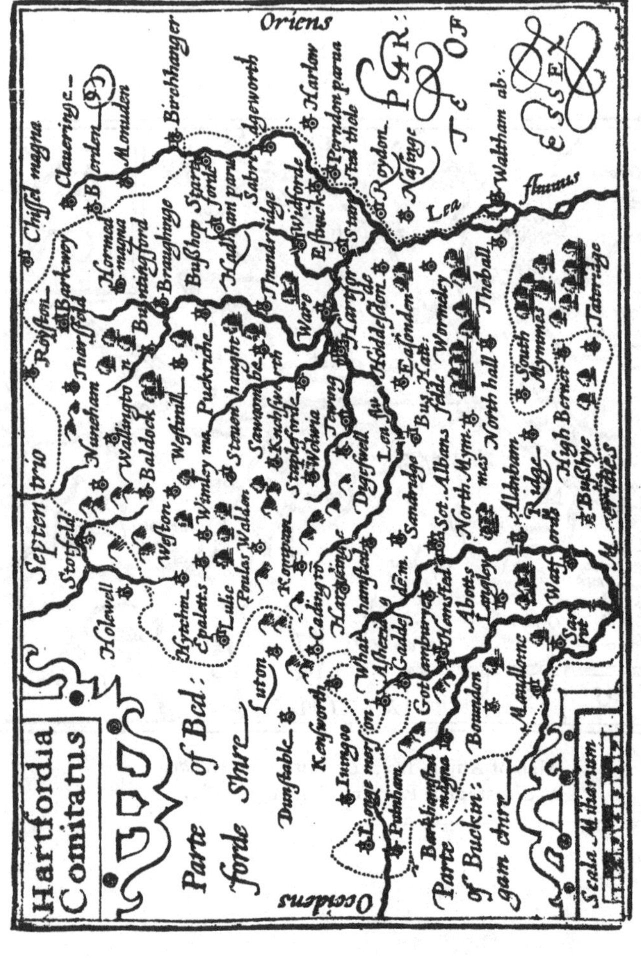

Map of Hertfordshire. Pieter van den Keere (1599)—(after Christopher Saxton, 1577). Amsterdam, 1617.

There was also published at Rome a yet earlier engraved map of the British Isles drawn by an Englishman, George Lily, and dated 1546.

The earliest set of provincial maps in our country is that of Christopher Saxton, making up 35 in number, but without any distinctive title. These maps were founded on an original survey, a great and difficult work. Some of them appeared as early as 1574 (Oxfordshire, Buckinghamshire and Berkshire in one map, and Norfolk). Kent, Hampshire, Dorset, Somerset, and Suffolk, are dated 1575, and the remainder 1576, 1577, and 1578. The whole collection appeared in 1579. It is very rare. A good copy might well be worth now more than £200, and it is curious to note the price in 1736, as recorded in John Worrall's *Bibliotheca Topographica Anglicana*, namely, 15*s*. Most of Saxton's maps were engraved by artists of the Low Countries. Van den Keere engraved a set of reductions of these maps which are not so rare as the originals. They are dated 1599. Saxton also published, about the year 1584, a large-scale general map of England and Wales, in twenty sheets, measuring, as a whole, 5½ feet in width, by 4½ feet in height, and on a scale which appears to be between 7½ and 8 miles to the inch. No copy of this map, in its original state, is known to exist. Our information on the subject is derived from a re-impression from Saxton's plates, much altered as to all the marginal and ornamental details, and with the roads added, by Philip Lea, whose version appeared in the reign of James II (about 1688). This continued to be sold up to at least the middle of the eighteenth century, but even this impression is extremely rare, five copies only having been identified. John Norden (1548–1625 or 1626) was next in succession to Saxton as an English cartographer. He invented the triangular, tabular statement of distances between towns still in use, but only issued maps of Middlesex (1593) and Herts (1598). He surveyed Hants, Surrey, Sussex, Cornwall, Essex and Northamptonshire and possibly Kent also. It was he who first inserted roads on our maps. In 1607 a folio edition of Camden's *Britannia* was issued, with maps by William Kip and William Hole, and in 1611 John Speed's *Theatre of the Empire of Great Britaine*, followed, later, by his *Prospect of the Most Famous Parts of the World*—a general atlas.

Towards the end of the seventeenth century appeared John Ogilby's *Britannia*—a set of folio drawings of the roads of England and Wales, arranged in strips, constructed from measurements with the wheel, or perambulator, on the basis of the statute mile, which then replaced the old British mile—the pre-Roman Gallic *leuga* of 1500 Roman paces, or 2200 modern mètres, as compared with 1760 yards, or 1609 mètres. The fact that this common measure of length throughout Central Europe subsisted, as the measure of distance on British roads, up to 1675, that is for at least 1700 years, is both curious and interesting.

John Ogilby's work laid the foundation of the long series of British and Irish Road-books and Road-maps, which continued to appear up to the period when traffic was largely diverted to our railways about 1850.

In the early part of the eighteenth century a number of maps and atlases were published in England by Seller, Senex, Moll, and Morden. These productions have little cartographic interest or originality, but were followed, in the latter half of the century, by a number of large-scale maps of the counties, published by subscription, from original surveys[1], while the rather indifferent work of the

[1] These surveys were based upon subscription, and were encouraged by the award of premiums and medals by the Royal Society of Arts. They were, naturally, costly to produce, and, in consequence, they exist only for the more residential counties, where the "nobility

Hartforde shire, Wth some cōfining Towns	Hertford	Ware	Hoddesdon	B. Stortford	B. Hatfielde	Puckeredge	Buntingford	Barkway	Royston	Baldocke	Hitchin	Hemsted	St Albans	Watford	Bernet	Barkhamsted	Tringe	Steuenedge	Welwyne	Theobaldes	Luton Bedf.	Dunstable Bed.	K. Langley	Market	Redbourne	Rickmansworth
Ivingoe Buc. W	19	20	22	28	15	22	20	24	23	26	12	7	11	13	20	4	3	15	13	24	7	5	9	6	7	13
Rickmansworth S.W	17	18	18	27	11	22	23	27	28	20	19	8	9	3	12	9	11	18	14	17	15	15	5	12	10	
Redborne W.	12	14	15	21	8	15	16	20	20	12	9	3	4	8	13	5	8	10	7	17	6	6	6	3		
Market W.	13	15	16	22	10	16	16	19	18	11	8	5	6	11	15	5	7	9	8	18	3	3	7			
K. Langley S.W.	14	16	16	24	9	19	20	23	24	17	14	3	5	4	12	5	8	14	11	17	10	10				
Dunstable Bed N.W	15	17	19	24	13	17	17	20	19	11	7	7	10	14	20	7	7	10	10	22	3					
Luton Bedf. N.W.	13	14	16	21	11	14	14	17	16	8	5	8	9	14	17	8	10	8	8	20						
Theobaldes S.E.	8	8	5	13	9	13	16	19	22	19	19	18	13	14	5	20	24	15	12							
Welwyne W.	5	7	9	14	5	8	9	13	14	8	8	7	6	12	11	12	15	4								
Steuenedge N.W	8	8	11	13	8	7	6	9	10	4	5	9	10	15	15	14	17									
Tringe S.W.	20	22	23	29	16	23	23	26	26	18	15	8	11	12	20	3										
Barkhāsted S.W	19	18	20	26	13	20	20	24	24	16	13	4	8	10	17											
Bernet. S.	9	10	8	17	7	15	17	22	23	18	18	14	10	9												
Watforde S.W	13	15	15	24	9	19	20	25	26	19	17	7	6													
St Albans S.W	10	12	12	20	5	14	15	19	20	13	11	5														
Hemsted S.W	14	16	17	24	10	17	18	22	23	15	12															
Hitchine N.W	12	13	16	18	12	11	10	12	12	4																
Baldock N.W	11	11	14	15	12	8	7	9	8																	
Royston N.	16	13	16	12	18	9	6	3																		
Barkway N.	14	11	14	9	16	6	4																			
Buntingford N	9	9	11	8	12	3																				
Puckeredge N	7	5	8	7	10																					
Hatfielde S.W	4	7	7	15																						
B. Stortford N.E	12	8	9																							
Hoddesde S.E	5	3																								
Ware N.E.	2																									

Cambrigshire North
Essex
East
Middelsex
South
Bedfo & Buckin: W

17

Table of Distances for Hertfordshire. London, 1635 and 1636.
From *A Direction for the English Traviller*.

Bowens (Thomas and Emanuel) and Thomas Kitchin became prominent in atlases of various scales.

About the year 1780, John Cary, who is perhaps the most representative, able, and prolific of English cartographers, began his work, which extended over more than 50 years[1]. His maps are of real beauty and delicacy. One of his assistants, Aaron Arrowsmith, also became well known as a cartographer.

In order to maintain my historic sequence, I now revert for a moment to the French cartographic effort of the eighteenth century. It was very marked and of great value to the progress of geographical accuracy and knowledge. The two de Lisles (Claude, 1644–1720, and Guillaume, 1675–1726) stand first in that century as exponents of exact cartography and were followed by d'Anville and others. It is not necessary to enumerate their contemporaries and successors, except to mention the *Atlas Universel* of the two Robert de Vaugondys which appeared in 1757 and the *Atlas Géographique et Militaire de la France*, published in 1751 by R. J. Julien. They mark the transition from speculative cartography, if it may be so-called, to that based on exact observation on the ground and the fixing of points by tri-

and gentry" were in a position to make up the subscription list. It appears that the map of Sussex, published in 1796, was estimated, in the prospectus, to cost more than £2400 for surveying, drawing and engraving, and to take six years in execution; four hundred subscribers at six guineas for the whole map were asked for. It is on the usual scale of these maps, namely two inches to a mile, is engraved on eight large sheets, and was published by William Faden, who received from the Society of Arts a premium of £50 for a map of Hampshire, and a gold medal for that of Sussex.

The first offer of prizes for County Maps by the Society was made in 1759, and these offers continue in the premium list up to 1801, while awards were made up to as late as 1809.

[1] See *John Cary, Engraver, Map, Chart and Print-Seller and Globe-Maker,* 1754 *to* 1835. A bibliography, with an Introduction and Biographical Notes, by the author. Cambridge, 1925, 4to.

angulation, the latter of these atlases being based on the great work of the Cassinis to which I now naturally refer.

This work was no less than the complete mapping on a scientific basis of the Kingdom of France, absorbing a period of labour of 45 years (1744–1789), and accomplished by César François Cassini de Thury (1714–84) and his son Jacques Dominique (1748–1845). The first sheet of this map (the *Carte Géométrique de la France*) appeared in the middle of the eighteenth century, just 50 years before the publication in England of the first one-inch sheet of our Ordnance Survey. Cassini's map is on a scale of $\frac{1}{86400}$ compared with ours of $\frac{1}{63360}$ and is made up of 180 sheets. A beautiful reduction to 24 sheets was published in 1789 by Louis Capitaine. To modern French cartography a slight reference will be made later. It presents no very special features. Some Italian maps of the end of the eighteenth century have already been noticed, to them also I shall again draw attention when I come to the discussion of technical details and art.

The various maps of our own Ordnance Survey are well known, and any general description would be superfluous. Our triangulation was commenced in 1783–4, when General Roy measured a base on Hounslow Heath. In 1787 a second base was measured, also by General Roy, in Romsey Marsh, from which the connection with the French triangulation was established in the same year. A complete map of the triangulation of that country had appeared in 1744.

Modern map production is an immense field, and it may be said to culminate in the World or International map, on the scale of one-millionth, in 2084 sheets, the first effort to obliterate the immense diversity of scales and technical methods which, up to now, has disfigured cartographic expression.

VII

SPECIAL MAPS.

Amongst maps having a special and limited object, it is proper that I should refer to geological maps, an important branch of cartography, if only in order to recall that it is to an English surveyor, William Smith, that we owe the first, and a most successful, attempt to establish knowledge of geological conditions by cartographic representation. Smith's surveys, and his maps published in the period 1815–1824, are wonderful for their general accuracy, and for their successful pictorial effect. They are all founded, as to geographical details, on the plates of John Cary, to whom I have already referred.

To those interested in great drainage areas the maps of the Great Level of the Fens are an object of study. A complete historical catalogue of the long series of maps connected with the Great Level appeared as an Appendix to my catalogue of the maps of the County of Cambridge, printed in the *Communications of the Cambridge Antiquarian Society* in 1908. Reference may be made to that work for information on the technique of maps of drainage-areas and their character and construction. The maps of the Great Level date from 1604, and those of special interest in size, detail, and cartographical importance are two—that of Sir Jonas Moore, 1684, and that of G. and J. Cary, prepared to illustrate Wells' *History of the Drainage of the Great Level of the Fens* and dated 1829.

Geological coast-line sections have a cartographic value, and should be mentioned. Generally coast-line panoramic views have been used as adjuncts to charts and in support of sailing-directions. The subject of panoramas and their relation to maps is left for discussion at a later stage of my general subject, but I should like to draw attention to the discovery some few years back of the sketch-book used on Drake's last voyage, in which a long series of coast outlines and views is recorded to enable future expeditions to successfully locate the Spanish ports and towns for purposes of attack. It was, it appears, the custom at that time to carry draughtsmen on the expeditions fitted out to harry the Spaniard, and this book is a beautiful example of the art so applied.

At the foot of the twenty-third drawing is a note of the death of the famous navigator and commander of the expedition, which has a profound sentimental and some historical interest:

> This Morninge when the discription notid or taken of this Lande beinge the 28. of Januarie 1595. beinge wedens daie in the morninge. Sr Frauncis Dracke Died of the bludie flix righte of the Ilande. de Buena Ventura. som. 6. Leagues at see whom now resteth with the Lorde.

Sea-charts, hydrographical surveys, and the plotting of soundings are not treated of here. The subject is, necessarily, an important one, but has little direct interest from the teacher's point of view, so far as ordinary elementary schools are concerned, at all events.

VIII

ART IN CARTOGRAPHY.

As curiosities of art in map production some ancient mosaic pavements and fresco drawings on the walls of temples must just be noticed, but they have no interest, other than historical, to the cartographer.

Tapestry maps have also a history of their own.

A monograph, descriptive, with illustrations, of the English tapestry maps of the sixteenth and seventeenth centuries, was published at the Victoria and Albert Museum in 1915. This publication is drawn upon to illustrate the subject so far as is necessary for my present purpose.

The maps described are said to represent the best energies of the weavers employed by William Sheldon of Weston and Barcheston in Warwickshire and Beoley in Worcestershire, and his descendants for several generations. Sheldon introduced tapestry as a native industry into England, though records of foreign weavers resident in this country exist from considerably before his time. He sent a workman over to the Netherlands to learn the craft in the middle of the sixteenth century, and, upon his return, looms were set up at Weston and Barcheston. William Sheldon himself died in 1570, some years earlier than the weaving of the earliest of the existing tapestry maps, the products of his looms. The surviving examples (except two fragments) are now in the Bodleian Library, or in the Museum of the Yorkshire Philosophical Society, and consist of seven complete, or nearly complete, maps of counties, or groups of counties, in central and southern England, and some fragments, which are carefully copied from contemporaneous engraved maps. They cover a period of manufacture of more than fifty years, commencing late in the sixteenth century, and illustrate the interest taken in local cartography at this period—the period of Saxton, Norden, and Speed.

Early in the last century it was sometimes the practice to work maps, on a small scale, with the needle. These maps are, of course, mere eccentricities.

The hand-colouring of engraved maps, and their adventitious ornamentation as well, which I now proceed to consider may, possibly, have had some connection with the portolan charts, which were drawn in colours.

In the latest examples, the Portuguese maps of the Reinels, the mainland both of Africa and South America is peopled with men and women and wild animals, dispersed in a luxuriant forest growth, and the whole is decorative in the highest degree. Ships sail the seas and marine monsters also abound.

These latter characteristics mark all the early efforts of the engraver, and, in addition, we find wide borders filled with figures and designs drawn to illustrate the dress and appearance of the inhabitants of the countries described on the maps. The science of the period is demonstrated in groups of astronomical and other instruments and apparatus, with floral designs, elaborate scroll work, and, in fact, at one time a map had as much space given to its marginal features as was reserved for actual cartographical delineation.

Comparisons may be made between the work of various engravers and designers, and between the artists of different countries and schools, but such comparisons would serve no useful purpose in this book.

It may be said of the earlier map-makers that, like nature, they abhorred a vacuum.

They made a practice of disguising their geographical ignorance by filling all blank spaces upon the maps themselves with designs of some sort—decorating the deserts with wild animals and fabulous monsters, and ornamenting the seas with ships and marine animals, thus following the portolan charts. This added enormously to the picturesque and gave a character of its own to the maps of the period.

Where all else failed, an elaborated system of intricate scrolls, forming part of names written on the maps and their margins, prevailed at one time—in the Dutch school particularly—but disappeared with the special Dutch cartographic art.

Map colouring was for a long period a regular profession. The celebrated Ortelius, to whom I have already referred, and who shares with Mercator the glory of the foundation of modern cartography, began his life-work by collecting and colouring maps for sale at Antwerp, where he was born. In the seventeenth century the art of illumination of maps was in so much repute that Jean Boisseau could describe himself (1636) as a court official, under the title *enlumineur du roi pour les cartes géographiques*, and another map-maker, Nicolas Berey, who worked for Nicolas Tassin, is, in 1641, *enlumineur de la reine*. Although colour was thus early applied to maps by hand, it was not until towards the end of the seventeenth century that this practice seems to have developed into an art. In the large folio atlases of the Jaillots, as, for instance, in the issue of 1696 (*Atlas Nouveau, contenant toutes les Parties du Monde*), this art is found in its most advanced form. From that time, however, it ceased to have any vogue, and the exact and scientific cartography of the eighteenth and following centuries does not appear to have ever lent itself to colouring for the embellishment of maps as works of art.

The atlas of the Jaillots is, in fine examples, coloured with great brilliancy, and in bright and striking, but, on the whole, successful contrasts. This brilliancy is sometimes enhanced by gilding. Of course, such examples are rare, as they must have been prepared specially at the cost of wealthy purchasers. Want of accuracy in conforming to the engraved outline frequently detracts from the value of this embellishment, but fine copies are well worth study from the point of view of decorative art.

There seems to have been no school of map illumination in England at any time, but, throughout the whole period anterior to the introduction of colour-printing, boundaries were outlined in colour by hand, and, towards the end of the eighteenth century, the general maps, as well as the numerous road-maps, are coloured, and with some success. Such delineation in colour is, of course, geographical, and not decorative. The use of colour in the former sense will be discussed later under the heading of technical characteristics of maps. Colour-printing and lithography hardly need any description as a part of the mechanics of map production.

When the art of engraving was first applied to cartography, the wood-block system was relied on; but this was soon displaced by the use of copper-plate, wood turning out but clumsy results in the delicate delineation necessary for clear expression of the details on maps.

Passing on from these primitive efforts it is realized that, for nearly three centuries, map-production depended entirely on copper-plate engraving, which has, up to about the middle of the nineteenth century, experienced but little competition from the use of other methods. Lithography, and, for more than a century past, the application of colour to engraved maps by similar processes have, however, come into current use, and we have now, in addition, photo-zincography as a means of inexpensive duplication. These methods have somewhat debased the art, as art, for, although the cheapness and accuracy of such processes make them of the highest utility, the appearance of maps and their artistic beauty are diminished by their use, and nothing really compares with the original impression from finely-engraved copper.

The earliest engraved maps having been printed from wood blocks, they must be referred to shortly.

They commence with the first printed map known to which a date can be assigned, that of 1490, published in Germany.

Another German publication, a Route-Map of Central Europe by Erhard Etzlaub, printed at Nuremberg in 1501, which is also from a wood-block, is very instructive. It has just been re-published, in facsimile, with a descriptive monograph. It measures 11¾ inches wide, by 16 inches high, is arranged with the south at the top, and follows exactly in outline, with all its errors, the Ptolemaic map of Germany. Colour is added, of course by hand, the sea being a dull green and mountain ranges brown. The towns are shown by small hollow circles, and the roads by dotted lines.

A third interesting example is the map of Italy, published in 1515 to illustrate Jacques Signot's guide to the ways and passages from France into Italy, written in connection with the movements of the French Armies in the wars which Charles VIII and Francis I carried on in the latter country. While the book itself is rare, the map, of which mention is made in the licence to print and publish, dated December 10th, 1515, was unknown, until I was fortunate enough to discover a copy in Paris, in a geographical exhibition selected from the treasures of the National Library, and to be able to identify it. A section from a photographic reproduction of this map is here engraved as a frontispiece (Plate I).

This map has an orientation diagonally across it, so that the top is about north-east. Towns are drawn pictorially on a large scale; the rivers are very prominent; the mountains are very clumsily shaded, and the sea is depicted covered with waves, while the various passes through the Alps into France and Switzerland are shown. It is of great interest, as an early example of the cartographic art in Europe. The copy in Paris was thought to be unique, but a second copy is now known to be in a private collection. Dark markings show the creasings of the map, as folded into the little quarto volume to which it belonged.

Another specimen of wood engraving as applied to cartography is the great map of France of François de La Guillotière, in nine sheets, which was published by Jean Le Clerc (probably in Paris) ornamented with elaborate addresses to the King, and to the reader, and was presented to Louis XIII in 1612, or 1613. It had taken sixteen years (1596–1612) in its preparation.

It is perhaps hardly worth while reviewing in any detail the development of the art of copper-plate engraving as applied to maps during the long period in which it has now flourished. It very early reached a high standard of excellence, especially in Amsterdam, where the Dutch engravers did some very fine, delicate and effective work, in the middle of the seventeenth century especially. The Blaeus are distinguished in this form of excellence. It may be said that prior to the middle of the century, the engraving of maps showed, in general, a certain coarseness of outline.

The engravers employed by Nicolas Sanson about the middle of the seventeenth century seem all to have come from the north of France, except Jean Somer, who described himself as *Pruthenus*, or the Prussian. Of them, R. Cordier is decidedly the finest artist. His minute delineations of buildings in profile, to represent towns of different sizes, bear magnifying with the glass and have a real charm. The five sheets in which Cordier has drawn in sections England and Wales are exceedingly beautiful. The ornamentation of the *cartouches* which decorate his plates is very simple and charming.

The large maps of the Jaillots, which are based upon the original and smaller plates of Sanson's atlases, are, apart from the colouring in special examples, very remarkable for

(A)

Plans of Fortresses in France and Flan

(B)

ders. Roch Joseph Julien. Paris, 1751.

the designs of the *cartouches* which present infinite variety, associated as the details are with the character and productions of the countries, or provinces, represented on the maps. Many of these designs are very elaborate, and some include portraits, plans of fortresses, and other details.

The two Robert de Vaugondys, for the engraving of their atlases of the eighteenth century, employed artists of much ability, and their maps, and particularly again the *cartouches*, are very charmingly designed. A map of France, by Julien, published in 1751, in sheets, is arranged so that, when put together as a single map, the border is made up of a complete series of small and beautifully-drawn plans of the French towns, with their respective coats-of-arms, and a short descriptive text. The angles of this border are filled with decorative panels, and, taking it as a whole, this is a fine specimen of decorative cartography. Nothing, however, attains to the beauty of the two large maps of the district and bay of Naples by Rizzi-Zannoni, already referred to as of the end of the eighteenth century. The surface of these maps is of marvellously minute execution, the panoramic representation of the coast-line on one of them especially is a lovely piece of work, and the borders and other ornamental features are superb.

Nearly contemporaneously with these Italian maps was published Capitaine's map of France already referred to. The texture, so to speak, of the engraved surface is worth very careful examination, and the large *cartouche* has much charm.

At this time John Cary was at work in England, and his productions in cartography were growing in delicacy of touch. It is later, towards the end of the cartographic activity of Cary and his successors, that his best work appeared: for example, a map of England and Wales in 65 large sheets, published in 1832.

The Teesdales produced some very fine work about the same time, as did the Greenwoods[1].

In the second half of the last century, map-engraving seems to have lost its beauty and originality, probably in view of the rigid uniformity of expression demanded of it. Here and there, however, especially in Switzerland, something of what I may call the purity of the engraved art remains.

This is a discursive review and only attempts to indicate salient points in progress, or decay. The world's output of maps in the last two centuries has been prodigious, and any exhaustive analysis of its art and technical development is almost impossible; and, were it possible, within any reasonable limits, would hardly be instructive from the teacher's point of view.

Finally, we have in the world-map, already more than once referred to, the latest state of colour and design applied in their simplest forms to cartography, with, it may be said, I think with truth, very satisfactory results.

There is one observation on the trend of decorative development which may be worth making. On examining

[1] Of county maps of England and Wales, of which there is a great series from the time of Saxton and Speed almost to our own day, the most ambitious, in the later period, are those of C. and J. Greenwood, for which the survey was begun about 1814, and continued until 1834. The Greenwoods had, of course, the ordnance survey sheets to work on. Their maps were on a scale of an inch to the mile, generally on four, or six, sheets, and were priced (with two or three exceptions) at three guineas each, the price of the whole set, in proof impressions, being 125 guineas. In a prospectus of May, 1824, it is stated that fifteen of the maps had been issued, and that it was expected that the survey would be completed "within the further period of about Six Years." It was, however, never actually finished, and the venture came to an end about 1830, when 34 maps (including S.E. Wales and London) had been issued, leaving, to complete the series, maps of Bucks, Cambs, Herefordshire, Herts, Norfolk and Oxfordshire.

a series of representative examples of engraved maps, from the time of Ortelius onwards, it will be noticed that the profuse and elaborate ornamentation to which I have referred as being remarkable in the maps of the early part of the seventeenth century, and the profusion of scattered drawings on the face of the maps themselves, gradually give way to a concentration of ornament almost exclusively in the angles of maps, in the form of the decorative panels, for which the French term *cartouche* is usually adopted, and which contain the titles of maps, the scales and other routine particulars.

I am sorry to say these *cartouches* have become a subject for the formation of collections; involving, of course, the destruction of masses of maps and atlases. This misplaced tribute to their artistic qualities is to be deplored in the interest of carto-bibliography, if of nothing else.

IX

HISTORY OF SPECIAL MAPS AND THEIR CLASSIFICATION.

(*a*) Road-Maps.

As I have already pointed out, the first object of the rudimentary map was travel. In the Middle Ages in Europe, the pilgrimages to the Holy Land, to Rome, and to local shrines, as for instance, St James of Compostella in Spain, and St Thomas of Canterbury and St Mary of Walsingham in England, became a development of systematic travel; and, in particular, the accounts of the great pilgrimage to Jerusalem of 1480, and others of about that period, which have come down to us in manuscript, or in print, show the continuation of the earlier military movement for the recovery of the Holy Land in a peaceful form well into the sixteenth century. It does not appear that any maps resulted directly from these journeys, but the land journeys from various points of Europe to Venice—the port of embarkation for Jaffa—are recorded by stages and thus form the foundation for the road-books, of which a large literature exists from the earliest systematic publications of this kind which appeared in the middle of the sixteenth century in France (1552) and a little later in England. Road-books were developed in England into road-maps, and this step in cartography spread later to the continent of Europe.

General road-maps are found as early as 1501 in Germany, and they have a considerable literature of their own from rather more than a century later.

War has at all times been productive of geographical study, but piety and commerce have been more dominant in producing results in this direction, probably, than even international conflict. The periodical fairs of the civilized countries were the foundation of commerce and the interchange of commodities, and, even before road-books appear, lists and tables of the fairs of Europe were in circulation, as well as tables of the numerous different coinages, and their comparative values. The whole of these materials of travel were brought together in guides and itineraries before 1600. Of the sea-maps of the Mediterranean I have already spoken. Their connection with modern charts is natural and close.

(*b*) War-Maps.

The classification of specialized maps would take up a long time in discussion. Here war and conflict dominate developments from early times and play a very large part in production. I do not know, however, of any maps which can be classed as *war-maps* earlier than the beginning of the

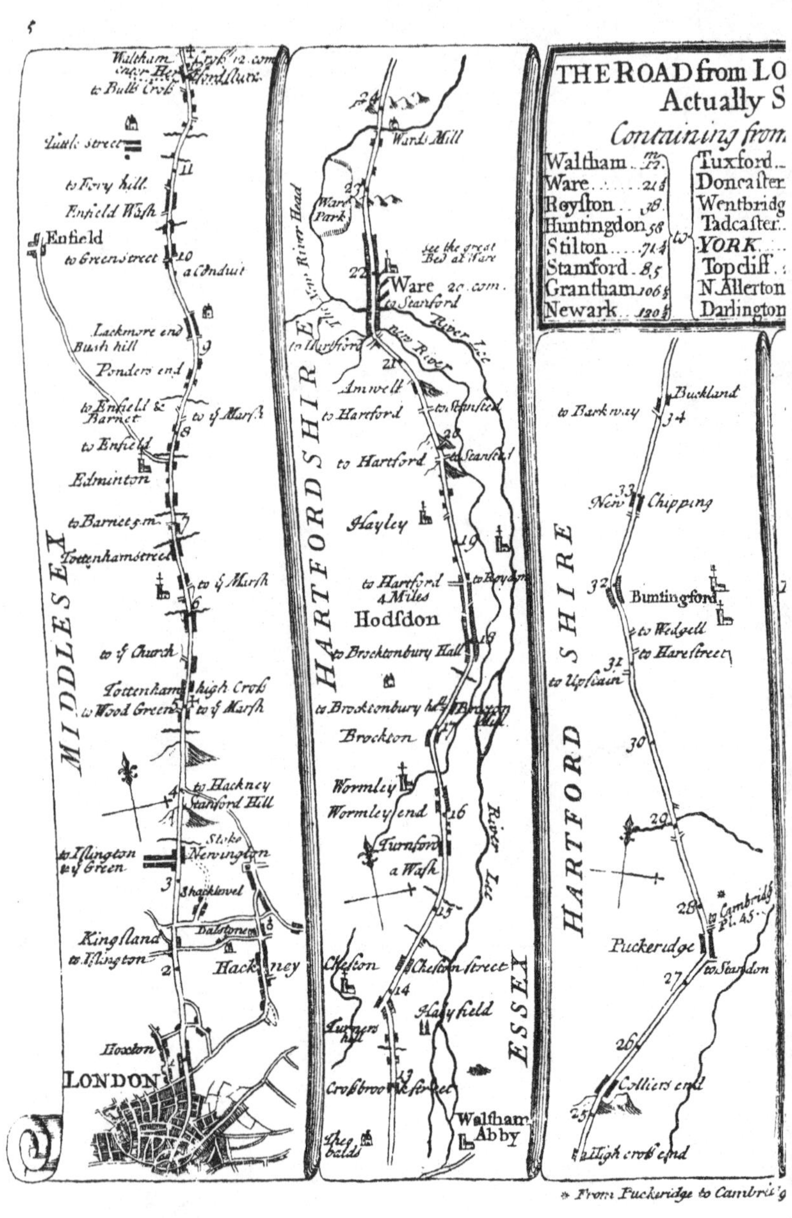

Road-strips. (After John Ogilby, 1675.)

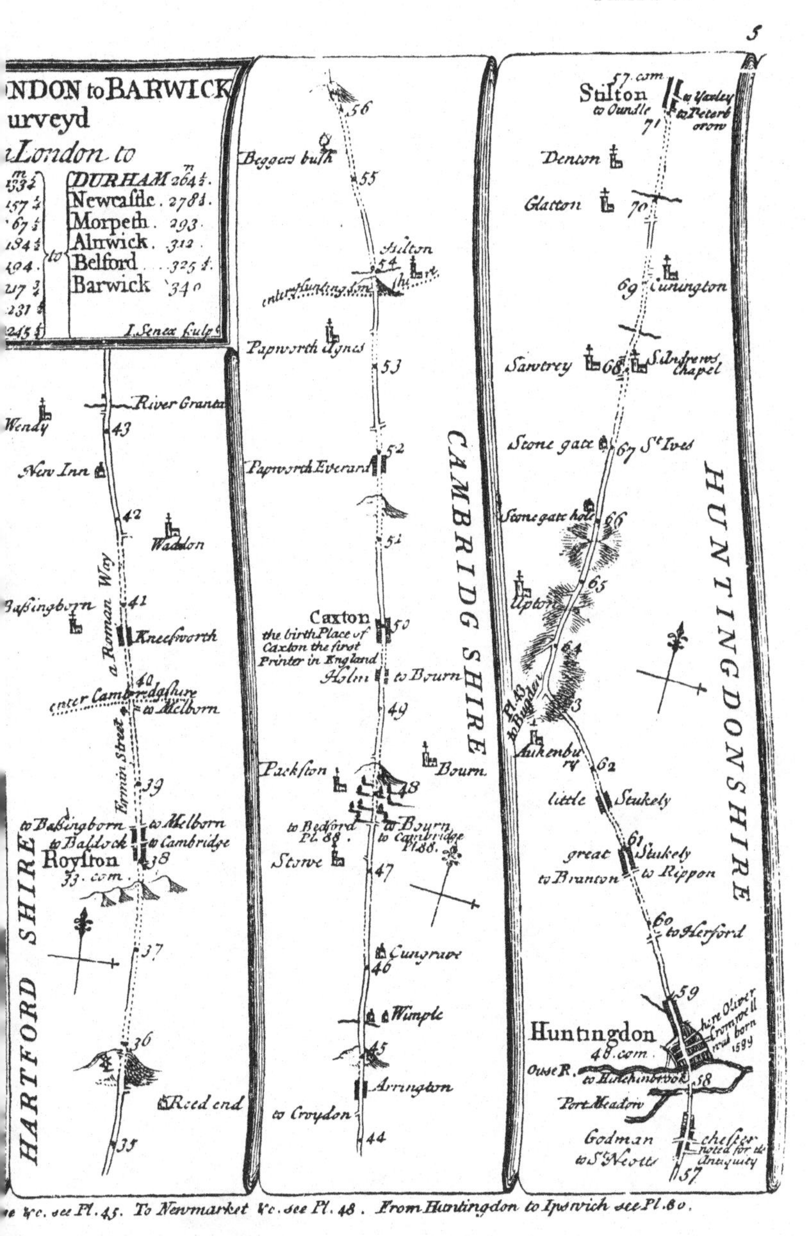

Reduced by John Senex. London, 1719.

seventeenth century, unless indeed we so classify a map of the Auvergne of 1560, by Symeone, which was drawn to illustrate a description of the struggle between Cæsar and Vercingetorix in the Gallic wars of 52 B.C., a map I refer to later as illustrating another point worth discussion. The final scene of this campaign will be remembered in the description Cæsar gives of the siege of the great entrenched camp of Vercingetorix at Alesia, in the north of Burgundy, and the defeat of the Gaulish relieving army which advanced upon his lines of circumvallation from the south. That victory, one of the momentous victories of the world's history, founded the Roman Empire.

Apparently the first of these war-maps are two found in Jean Le Clerc's *Théâtre Géographique du Royaume de France*, about 1619. One represents, in a very pictorial form, the military movements in the struggle between Henry IV and the League round Paris. On this map the Battle of Ivry (14th March 1590), the sieges of Corbeil and Lagny, and the march of the Spanish forces from the Netherlands on Paris under Alexandre Farnese, Prince of Parma, are shown. The map is very rare, and is much prized by collectors. It is neither signed nor dated. The other map shows the siege of St Jean d'Angely: *Assiegé par Louis* 13e *Roy de France et de Navarre, et rendu le* 25e *Juin* 1621. This is signed by Jean Le Clerc and dated in the same year.

Melchior Tavernier drew, in 1627, several maps to illustrate the siege of La Rochelle, and the movements, naval and military, in the Isle of Rhé, including the retreat of the English Army after the assassination of Buckingham. He also published in his *Théâtre Géographique* some charming sketches of the naval operations on the Mediterranean coast of France against the Spanish forces.

We may recall, with a mild glow of patriotic satisfaction.

that one of the most beautiful, and one of the earliest applications of cartography to recording battles at sea, is that of Robert Adams, "Surveyor of the Queen's Buildings," who prepared and published in 1590, presumably for Lord Howard of Effingham, the Lord High Admiral, eleven charts, depicting the successive engagements in the Channel in 1588 between the English Fleet and the Spanish Armada, from the invaders' first appearance thirty miles south-west of the Lizard, and throughout their progress to the coast of France and to their last and most damaging defeat off Gravelines, near Calais; the series closing with a general chart of the seas round the British Islands, showing the course taken by the Spaniards until, coasting round the north of Scotland and Ireland, they at last departed on their tempestuous retreat to Spain.

These charts were engraved from Adams' drawings by Augustine Ryther, a young Yorkshireman settled in London, who had previously been employed on the title-page and four of the maps (Durham, Gloucestershire, Westmorland and Yorkshire) of Saxton's set of county maps of 1579[1].

Tavernier also published maps of the Valtelline, connected with the struggle for the right of passage between Germany and Italy upon which depended the power of drawing upon German mercenaries for the carrying on of the Italian wars.

Later, we find the plans of fortresses and the delineation of sieges largely developed, and drawn with great skill by military engineers, showing the trenches and approaches, the batteries and their range, and many other military details. These cartographic efforts anticipate by more than two centuries the remarkable maps of the trench lines in

[1] Ryther's charts have recently been reissued in facsimile, printed at the Chiswick Press, for the Roxburghe Club (London, 1919).

France in the late war, founded on aerial observation and photography. The maps supplied to the staffs of the allied armies, as constructed during the operations, are really marvellous in their detail and exactness.

The records of movements of armies and fleets on maps may probably date from about the end of the seventeenth century only. At all events there exists a map of the Low Countries showing all the movements extending over four or five years in the campaigns of 1691–1695, which is a good example of this kind of cartographic expression.

Naturally the modern war-map is a necessary adjunct of military and general history.

(*c*) Geological and other Specialized Maps.

The history of geological maps does not extend over much more than a century, commencing with the work of William Smith in 1815, already mentioned. Some slight attempt had been made earlier, however, to indicate on maps geological and mineralogical conditions, as, for instance, on a map of Paris, published in the *Indicateur Fidèle*, 1764, a French road-book, where there is a table of signs, as used on the map, nineteen in number, distinguishing various mineralogical conditions. Finally, climatic conditions, and the winds and currents of the ocean, have been largely plotted on maps, and various systems of curves have been similarly used. Daily weather-maps and charts are the last development of this form of cartography.

The 'Times' Atlas of the World, published a few years back, contains interesting specimens of these branches of the science. Amongst them are four maps of the British Isles: one is a Bathy-orographical map, on a scale of two-millionths, showing the heights of land at levels of 250, 500, 1000, 2000,

3000, and 4000 feet, and depths of the sea of 10, 20, 30, 40 and 50 fathoms, distinguished by colour layers; another shows vegetation and climate, classified as to the former in grass and cultivated land, woodland, and moorland, hill pasture, etc.; this map has insets for (1) temperature, and (2) rainfall. The third of these maps deals with railways and industrial features, and the fourth is political, with insets showing industrial conditions and density of population.

These are good examples of maps constructed with very specialized objects, but, of course, a very long list of such maps could be prepared. We have, amongst others, modern maps drawn to show national, racial and political boundaries.

X

PANORAMAS AND THEIR RELATION TO MAPS.

Panoramic views have a close relation to maps. In mountainous country, where considerable elevations are available, a circular photograph can be taken which has a close resemblance to a map, and between this representation of surface and the distant view of a mountain range, or a cliff line, there is an infinity of gradations.

In early maps there was a disposition to combine plan and profile. I may cite as an example the map already mentioned of a part of the Auvergne, in France, drawn by a Florentine, Gabriel Symeone, and published in 1560 (Plate VII). It is a small, circular map, with the west at the top. At the foot, on an eminence, in the foreground, so to speak, is depicted an engineer, or cartographer, with his books and instruments, who appears to be making a survey. Behind him his servant is holding his horse. On either side are hills, and the distance is framed in hills. The body of the design shows

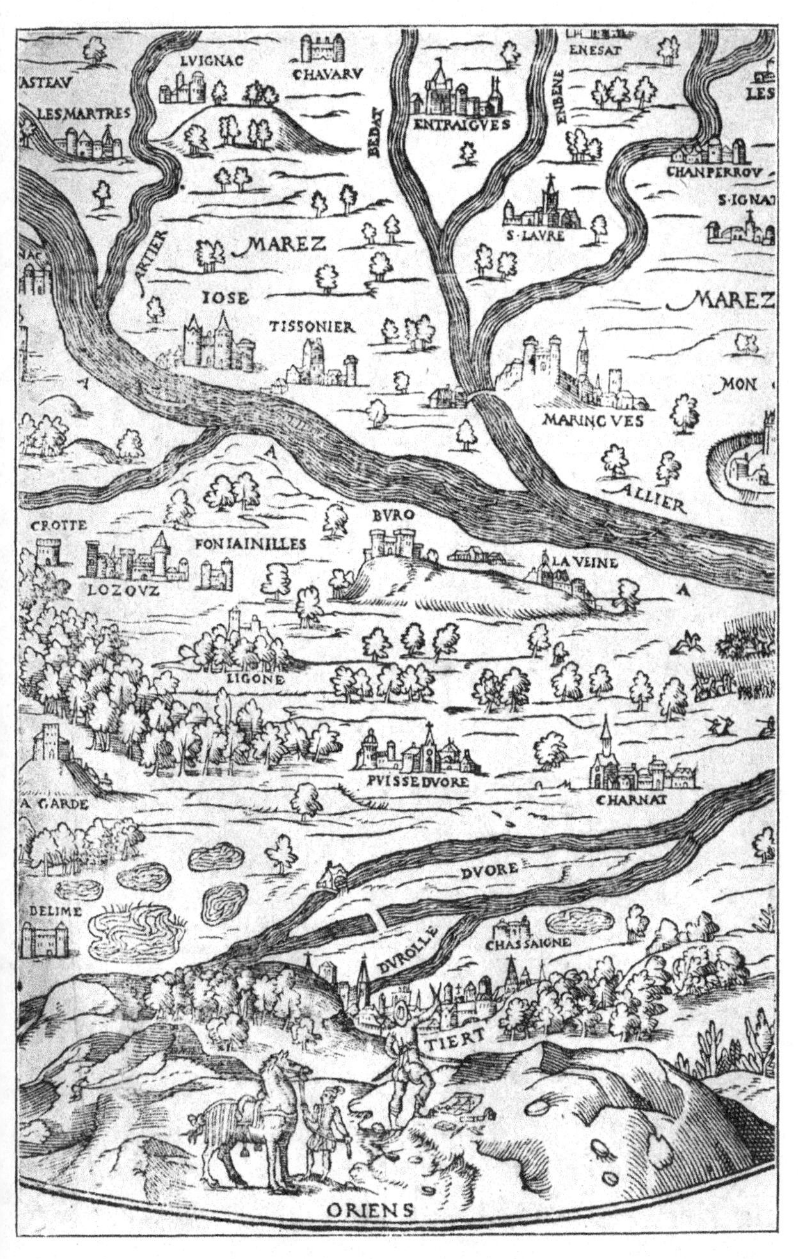

Section from Map of the Auvergne. Gabriel Symeone. Lyons, 1560.

the plain and course of the River Allier and its tributaries. This method of representation of surface was soon disused, but it is revived in the latter part of the seventeenth century in the plans and views of the fortresses of Europe which at that time were engraved in considerable number in connection with the elaborate system of defence adopted by the well-known military engineer, Vauban, who flourished at this period. As an example of this combination of plan and profile in dealing with the maps of fortifications and of the surrounding country, the numerous sheets and plates of fortified towns and places inserted in the great atlas of the Jaillots, edition of 1696, by the Amsterdam editor Mortier, are interesting. In the same atlas are plans and profiles of Namur and of the siege by King William III, in 1695, which ended in the capture of the town, after an attack which lasted ten months.

In the Alps panoramic sketches have long been in vogue, and, more recently, photography has enabled very beautiful results to be achieved. The panorama from the summit of Mt Blanc, and similar views of the main chain of the Alps from the Diablerets and other heights, are very striking and interesting.

I am inclined to think that, from the teacher's point of view, the judicious use of this material would give good results, and enlarge the general conceptions of the map itself.

There is poetic inspiration in looking out from mountain heights over the fertile plain, or a distant expanse of sea. Amongst the brilliant and artistic posters distributed in Alsace and Lorraine since these provinces reverted to France, is one showing the French soldiers in the trenches on the eastern slopes of the Vosges, looking with longing eyes on the great Plain of the Rhine Valley—a placard enriched with the words of Victor Hugo: *Le ciel est notre azur*,

Ce champ est notre terre! Cette Lorraine et cette Alsace, c'est à Nous! and a dream-picture, in the skies, of the great Cathedral of Strasburg.

The panorama of a coast-line has been used by stratigraphical geologists to fix and illustrate the lie of geological formations. I have also already referred to the use of such delineation by early navigators, and it remains, by way of marginal note, a regular feature of sea-charts and books of sailing directions. The soldier is trained in modern warfare to translate, with the aid of sketches, range-finders, and actual measurements, the panorama which is in his view from any defensive position into the map-form of a range-card and other records of distance and direction as laid down on a flat surface.

XI

THE ESSENTIAL ELEMENTS OF MAPS.

(*a*) Scales and their History.

It is not proposed to discuss here the history of scales on maps prior to the Middle Ages in Europe.

Scales are, however, found on the portolan charts. Stevenson, in his book already noticed, says: "A scale of miles divided into fifths or tenths is usually drawn on these charts, often in as many as four or five different places, and frequently on charts of later years in a very elaborate *cartouche*. It is often very evident that the drafting of such a scale was not done with careful attention to accuracy. Uzielli is of opinion that it was the Roman mile of 1481 mètres which was generally taken as the unit of measurement."

He also notes that the same scale does not appear to have

been employed for the Atlantic coast as was used for the Mediterranean, and this fact seems to explain the frequent distortion of the coast regions lying beyond the Straits of Gibraltar, and other errors.

On engraved maps, scales are found from the beginning. The Latin expressions of measurements of these scales show great variety: "Milliaria Gallica communia"; "Scala Milliariorum"; "Scala Leucarum Gallicarum"; "Milliaria Pictonica communia et magna"; "Scala Leucarum," and many other forms can be found on the small number of maps from various sources collected in the *Théâtre François* of 1594, and any atlas of the first century of the production of engraved maps shows the same, or even greater, variety. On the map of Blaisois in this series—there dated 1591—an explanation of the scale is given and the league is stated to be 25 to a degree, making the equatorial measurement of the globe 9000 leagues. In every province of France there seems, prior to the Revolution of 1789, which brought about uniformity of measurements, to have been a larger and a lesser league, and sometimes a middle or mean league between the two. Of course every country of Europe had its own national measures of distance then, as many have them still. Nautical miles, the reader will remember, differ considerably from similar land measures of distance, creating a further possibility of confusion in the combination of land and sea on a map. It is hardly necessary to notice that the Irish mile and the Irish acre do not correspond at all with the measures so denominated in Great Britain.

The road-map of Germany of 1501, already noticed, has a scale along the whole bottom border, making up 210 German miles, being the width of the map.

The maps of Ortelius, Mercator, and their successors, down to modern times, show, associated with their engraved scales, artistic designs in the form of decorative panels, with open compasses and other instruments of measurement.

The group of twenty different scales engraved on one of the sheets of Julien's map of France of 1751 is a good example of the great variety of standards of measurement which a cartographer of as late as the middle of the eighteenth century thought it necessary, or at least desirable, to engrave in explanation of a single map.

There are two methods in use in the expression of the scale of a map. We are accustomed in this country to refer everything to miles on the surface delineated expressed in inches, or proportions of inches, on the map itself. This is a realistic and convenient method. It appeals to the eye, and enables one to measure off on a map distances in miles by the use of any ordinary rule divided into inches. It does not, however, find favour elsewhere, and maps in this country, on anything like a large scale, now show that scale as a fraction, as well as on the basis of the "miles to an inch" expression. Thus for a map on the scale of 1 inch to 1 mile, being on that of 1 inch to 63,360 inches, the scale is written $\frac{1}{63360}$. The scales on our ordnance maps will be found set out and explained—with all the other technical details—in the thin folio publication of the Survey, sold at 6*d*., which deals exhaustively with these matters, and should be in the hands of every teacher of geography. These scales are:

General Maps	1 inch to 1 mile = $\frac{1}{63360}$
County Maps	6 inch scale = $\frac{1}{10560}$
Town Plans	Scale = $\frac{1}{500}$
Parish Plans	Scale = $\frac{1}{2500}$

At the end of this publication, specimen reproductions of these maps, with the various colourings, shadings, etc., adopted (eleven in all) are given.

Abroad, the fractional expression of scale is used, and this method is naturally associated with the decimal and metrical systems there in vogue.

The World, or International, map on the scale of one-millionth, $\frac{1}{1000000}$ may be read 1 millimètre to 1 kilomètre in English fashion. The 2084 sheets are to be drawn in gores, so that, when put together they will form a globe one-millionth of the earth's size, which will be found to be a little over 42 feet in diameter. If reduced to the English "miles to the inch" scale, this may be described as of 15·76 miles to the inch.

It marks an epoch in map-making. The project was first suggested in 1891 and was under continuous discussion amongst experts until matters were brought to a point at the Geographical Congress held at Geneva in 1908, when the delegates of the United States proposed that arrangements should be made to standardize the map, a proposition which was agreed to unanimously. An official International Committee met in London in November 1909, and this Committee and a Conference held in Paris in 1913 finally settled the numerous technical questions which are the foundation of this immense undertaking.

Of the estimated number of sheets for the world as a whole, 1920 are accounted for grouped in six continental and two oceanic "blocks," with the polar regions in addition. Approximately 974 sheets of the continental "blocks" contain land. The sheets already published are 212 in number, but of these only 26 conform to the Regulations promulgated by the Paris Conference of 1913; 103 are not in accordance with those Regulations, but have layer tints shown upon them, and 83 are provisional editions only, without layers. In addition, 12 new sheets are in proof stage, and 59 in preparation, and there are besides in preparation

6 new editions of sheets already published. The above are the statistics of progress contained in the official Report of the Central Bureau (Southampton) for the year 1926, which has just appeared. This Report is illustrated by a map upon which this progress is graphically shown. It is certainly to be regretted that the conventions of 1913, upon which the world-uniformity of the sheets depend, have not been more rigorously adhered to, but, nevertheless, as will be seen, substantial progress has been made, and the general idea receives every year wider recognition.

It will be realized by teachers how much is involved in, and how much may be learned from, this important departure in cartography, of which, perhaps, it is not too much to say that the adoption of a *world-scale* is one of the most striking features.

It is, perhaps, worth bearing in mind that the practice of grouping together, either on the walls of a school, or in the book form of an atlas, a number of maps drawn on very different scales may well lead to serious errors in the minds of children, or even of adults, in the conception of relative size in countries and continents. The teacher should, therefore, impress upon his class the importance of understanding the scale of every map from which instruction is drawn.

(*b*) Orientation.

The orientation of a map is purely conventional, but it is essential to the right reading of maps that some conventional system of "placing" a map, or a single sheet of a map in relation to the surface of the earth itself, and to other maps, or sheets, should be universally observed.

The Romans and Arabs drew maps with the south at the top. The same arrangement may be noticed in the German route-map of 1501. Early mediæval maps were drawn with the east at the top, with, sometimes, above the border, a representation of Paradise. The Holy Sepulchre at Jerusalem seems also to have had a religious, or sentimental, influence on the orientation of maps in Europe at a time when scientific opinion can hardly be said to have existed. Until quite late in the eighteenth century it was the uniform practice of English cartographers to indicate the east by a cross, in deference to, or at least in perpetuation of, the influence on orientation of the Christian veneration for the sacred places of the east, and finally, it is to be noted that the very technical expression "orientation" is derived from this looking to the east.

Towards the end of this long period of obscurity in fixing the direction in maps, the Italian and Catalan navigators, working with the compass, established a northern orientation for their charts.

It is not until 1532 that we find a printed chart upon which the variation of the compass is represented, this being Ziegler's map of Palestine, and not until 1595 is the declination represented on a marine chart.

The variation of the compass is now shown on such charts, and on the margins of our ordnance maps, and generally on large-scale maps in ordinary use. It need hardly be said that close attention is given to this matter by soldiers in relation to direction on maps, and particularly in dealing with the co-ordination of the movements of units at night.

The early idea of direction seems to have been associated with the prevalent winds. The north was Boreas, the west was Zephyrus, and the number of winds, that is directions, was increased in time to eight, and then to sixteen. The compass-roses on French and Italian maps and charts illustrate this arrangement, as may be seen on Julien's map of France of 1751, and on the map of the Bay of Naples of 1793 by Rizzi-Zannoni.

Any departure from the present settled convention that

maps are universally drawn with the top towards the north is very disconcerting, as may be realized by an inspection of the maps in a little book in two volumes, *The Picture of England*, published by a certain William Green in 1804, in which, for what reason is not stated, all, or nearly all, the maps are drawn, as we should say, upside down.

The various graphic methods, from a simple arrow-head to an elaborate and ornamental design, by which cartographers have represented the direction of the points of the compass on maps, afford a large field of study from the artistic and conventional standpoints. It would be possible to make a collection including an infinite number of designs from the earliest days to our own times, but the student of maps from the geographical side is not much concerned with this matter, and I do not propose now to pursue it further.

(*c*) Location.

Ideas as to measurement of the earth's surface and the setting out of lines of latitude and longitude come down to us from very early days, but they were subject to renewed discussion in the Middle Ages in Europe—dark ages they were as regards scientific exactitude.

As to the latitude, there seems to have been no difficulty, but the position to be assigned to the initial meridian of longitude gave rise to prolonged discussion, which can hardly be said to be terminated even to-day, though the fact that the International Map is based on the meridian of Greenwich Observatory seems to fix that initial point as established without contest for the future.

The cartographers of the sixteenth and seventeenth centuries accepted, under the influence of the Ptolemaic tradition, an initial meridian passing through the Azores, or the Canary Islands. Martin Cortes, in his book, published at

Seville in 1556, and of which the English translation appeared in London with the title *The Arte of Navigation* five years later, lays down the rule that for a first meridian of longitude we should draw a vertical line "through the Azores, or nearer Spain, where the chart is less occupied." Christopher Saxton's large general map of England and Wales, of about 1584, is drawn on an initial meridian of the Island of Saint Mary, the most easterly of the group of the Azores. Then we find the celebrated navigator John Davis stating in his black-letter pamphlet of 1594, entitled *The Seamen's Secrets*, that the first meridian passed through St Michael, because there was no variation at that place, the meridian passing through the magnetic pole as well as the geographical pole of the earth; but, of course, the identity of the magnetic meridian with any particular meridian at a given time was an entirely unsound basis for fixing the first meridian of longitude, as the variation of the north by the compass from the true north at any point on the earth's surface is not constant. In 1581 the variation at London was 11° 15′ E.; in 1657 there was no variation there, and it moved westerly until 1815, when it was 24° 27′ W., and is now returning eastwards. The variation of the magnetic from the true north in 1910, as recorded on sheet 24 of the ordnance map on the scale of 2 miles to 1 inch, or $\frac{1}{126720}$, was 16° 1′ W., with a non-constant decrease of 6′.

Following Davis, and a little later, Camden discusses this matter in his address to the reader, which is the preface to his edition of the *Britannia* of 1607, as translated by Philemon Holland for the first English folio edition (1610). After remarking on the general agreement as to latitude, he goes on: "But in the longitude there is no accord, no consent at all. What should I then do? When as therefore the modern navigators have observed that there is no variation in the Compasse at the Isles of Azores, I have thence begun with them, the account of longitude as from the first meridian, which yet I have not precisely measured."

The Island of St Michael mentioned by Davis is the largest of the group of the Azores; from its western extremity London should be 25° 54′ E., the island extending east and west between 25° and 26° W. of Greenwich.

In Herman Moll's *Atlas Manuale*, published in 1709, is a dissertation, in the introduction, on the "Correction of Longitude by Modern Observation," and a table showing the true longitude from London, by observation, and the differences between the longitudes of a number of principal cities, etc., in the world, as taken from London, Teneriffe, and Ferro respectively, and the longitudes as "Erroniously Plac'd in the Common Maps." These extracts are sufficient to show that much doubt and variety of opinion existed for a long period upon this subject, vital as it was to the accuracy of cartography.

To sum up this confusion, it seems that the Spaniards and Portuguese reckoned from the line of demarcation (370 leagues west of the Cape Verde Islands) sanctioned by the Pope, and that the Protestant Dutch, Germans and English at first went back to Ptolemy, who began at the Canaries. Mercator, on his globe of the year 1541, chose the Island of Forteventura in the Canaries for his initial meridian, but he afterwards adopted Corvo in the Azores. Ortelius, Janson, and Blaeu fixed on the Isla del Fuego in the Cape Verde group, and later, Blaeu proposed the Peak of Teneriffe, and in this he was followed by the Dutch. In France, in 1634, Richelieu, after consultation with the astronomers Gassendi and Morin, by decree of Louis XIII fixed upon Ferro (*Ile de Fer*), the most westerly of the Canaries, and enacted that all French ships should calculate their longitudes from this initial meridian, though it was not till the close of the seventeenth century that a French expedition determined with accuracy the relation of the position of Ferro to that

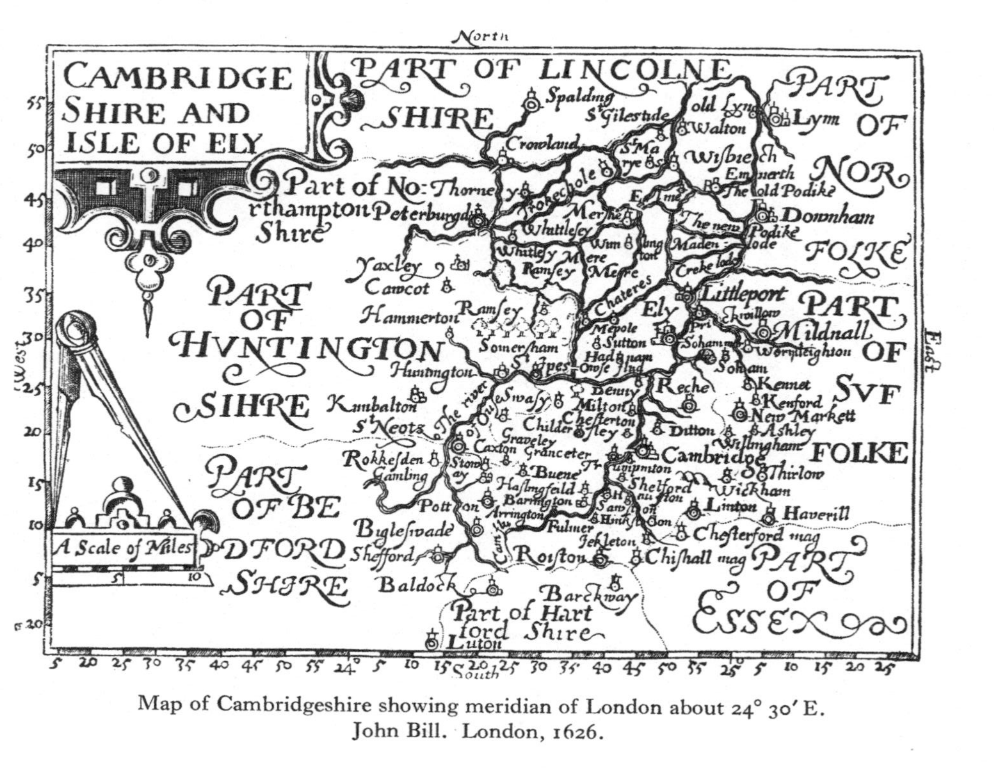

Map of Cambridgeshire showing meridian of London about 24° 30′ E.
John Bill. London, 1626.

of the observatory of Paris. It was in this way that the Ferro meridian obtained almost universal currency down to the beginning of the nineteenth century.

The vague western meridian was continued in use in England until towards the end of the seventeenth century. In Blome's *Britannia*, published in 1673, there is a map of the British Isles engraved by Francis Lamb and dated 1669, in which London is placed on a meridian line of 20° 30′ E., which seems to be based on a point on one of the most westerly of the Canaries rather than through the Azores, though an accurate measurement would lie between those two groups of islands.

In John Seller's map of Hertfordshire, dated 1676, the meridian of London first appears in use, as far as I have been able to ascertain. It was from that date uniformly used on English maps, until about the end of the next century, and, when fixed more exactly, the meridian is drawn through St Paul's Cathedral. This was displaced in its turn by Greenwich Observatory. John Cary, in his county atlas of 1787 (*New and Correct English Atlas*), and the second edition of 1793, bases all his maps on the meridian of London, but in the year following the latter date, on June 11th, 1794, he issued his *New Map of England and Wales, with part of Scotland* in 81 sheets, drawn on a scale of 5 miles to the inch, and upon this map, for, it seems, the first time, appears the meridian of Greenwich, associated, no doubt, with the fact that the Ordnance Survey triangulation, commenced in 1783, had then made substantial progress. It will be seen, therefore, that, as regards initial meridians in England, we have three periods: (i) of the old vague meridian in the Atlantic, which ended with the adoption of London about 1676; (ii) of the meridian of London itself, 1676 to 1794, and (iii) of that of Greenwich, which has now received the sanction of the international convention for the preparation of the World Map.

XII

GRAPHIC EXPRESSION OF SURFACE.

In the conventional and pictorial representation on a map of features of the earth's surface there is an obvious classification into (1) natural and (2) artificial. In the first we deal with the distinction between sea and land, the course and character of rivers, lakes, mountain and plain, and areas covered with ice, with sand, with marsh lands and natural forests, and the superficial aspects of rock stratification. In the second we place roads, buildings (isolated or in groups), canals, ports, bridges, and, on modern maps, railways, and telegraph and telephone lines. In the artificial features connected with the work of man on the earth there is infinite variety for systematic treatment in cartography. The natural features are obviously more constant.

To discuss first the natural features and the methods adopted for their delineation on maps.

The ideal here is to construct maps in actual relief; but such maps, which have, of course, a high instructional value, are, unfortunately, very costly to produce, and cumbersome to preserve. They involve a complete system of contours as a basis, in themselves an expensive feature of map construction.

Upon such a basis they can be easily built up in simple geographical areas, by using sheets of cardboard of the thickness equivalent, on the vertical scale adopted, to the distance vertically between contours. Such cardboard, cut to the areas included within a contour, or slightly larger, can be glued down on the map, as a practical adaptation of the layer system as usually indicated by colour. These layers are superimposed successively, and the edges of the sheets can then be pared down with a knife.

The defect in relief maps is the same as is constant in geological sections, namely, the enormous divergence between the vertical and horizontal scales. This is, of course, inevitable, but it is difficult of realization to the uninstructed pupil, and must be made clear in using such maps in teaching.

Contours are of modern use only. They follow the surface as lines of equal altitude above an agreed level—usually the mean sea-level at some standard point. The first idea of their value in surface representation is said to date back to 1729, when a Dutch surveyor drew lines of equal soundings in this manner. Later, Philippe Buache made use of the same system for delineating the form of the sea bottom in the English Channel. Contour lines were employed for land surfaces towards the end of the eighteenth century, especially in military plans, where the relative command of ground is of great importance, and they were more generally adopted in France, on the suggestion of Laplace, in 1816; but, only four sheets of this kind of map had been published up to 1833. In 1831 an attempt was made to work contour lines, "in the French mode," on the survey maps of Ireland, but it was not until twelve years later that the value of contouring had become officially recognized and was generally adopted in both Great Britain and Ireland, after a pronouncement in its favour had been made at the British Association meeting at Cork in 1843. Perhaps the most interesting examples of the conjoined use of contours and hill shading are found in the Swiss *Atlas Siegfried*, where the lines are 30 mètres apart in altitude.

The layer system is that of applying colours in a settled series of tones to the contours, so as to produce a solid appearance.

Contours and layers can both be adapted equally well to depth of water below as to height above sea-level.

Hill shading, on the principle of drawing fine lines from the top of an elevation to delineate the direction down which water would naturally flow from the highest point, or ridge, in a number of rivulets, is of some antiquity. The successful application of this system depends on conventional ideas as to the point, or points, from which light falls on the map. In adopting such a system there are obvious difficulties which the examination of a series of maps engraved on the *hachure* method would at once make clear.

The smaller-scale map of Switzerland, known as the *Carte Dufour*, is a good example of this method.

Some maps of mountainous districts in central Europe, engraved in the seventeenth century, have rather a grotesque appearance, where one uniform shading on the same side of every eminence in a large group of mountains has been developed.

The sea and other areas of water have been differently treated. The Dutch map-makers adopted, in the beginning of the seventeenth century, a uniform design of conventional waves over the whole water surface, which gave the map a very heavy appearance, but had the advantage of bringing the land surface into strong relief. This method did not survive the advent of the French school, as Nicolas Sanson left water without decoration. A modern arrangement is to distinguish water by drawing a series of very fine lines parallel to the coast-line to cover a uniform distance from the land. Sea and inland waters are now generally tinted in shades of blue, and the same colour is used for rivers, reservoirs and canals.

Ice- and snow-fields and glaciers are left white on maps. On the Swiss maps the contour lines on snow or ice are uniformly drawn in blue, while they are black on moraines and bare rock, and of a reddish-brown on ordinary pasturage and surfaces. Woods and forests are, on large-scale maps, represented by the drawing of minute trees. In the Dutch maps, and the maps generally of the earlier period of engraved cartography, the woods are shown in a very clumsy manner, and with trees grotesquely large. Areas of blown sand (*dunes*) have been for a long period represented graphically by undulating lines.

In the representation of artificial features, we find in the early maps much pictorial effect. On the French wood-cut map of 1515 the cities of Rome and Venice are drawn pictorially—to the size of a half-crown—and this practice is followed in later maps, in France especially, though an inset plan of the principal town on a map is adopted in French maps by the end of the sixteenth century, thus avoiding the absurdity of enormously exaggerating the town on the map itself.

Sanson's maps are distinguished by very finely drawn and varied outlines of churches, towers, and groups of buildings, arranged with some relation to the size and population of the towns thus represented. These little sketches are so fine and delicate that they repay individual study with a magnifying glass.

Smaller centres of population are early represented by a drawing, quite out of proportion also, of the church as the central and characteristic building. Roads do not, except in a few cases which have already been referred to, appear on maps earlier than the latter part of the seventeenth century. Later they become a usual feature, and distinction is made between various classes of roads, by the use of double, single, and in some cases, broken lines.

Bridges and fords naturally appeared on maps before roads, as they enabled travellers to shape out their general course, even in districts where roads themselves were either non-existent or mere trails.

Abbeys, and monastic buildings, were also indicated at an early stage of systematic map-making, perhaps in view of the hospitality they offered to the wayfarer, rather than from any special devotional sentiment, though the latter may have had some influence.

It does not fall within the scope of a hand-book to enumerate and describe all the mass of technical details which appears on our maps to-day. It is not, however, to be assumed that the subject is not of importance. It is the foundation of map-reading, and has an instructional value of its own in adapting the mind to the comparative study of the map and the actual surface it represents.

The earliest engraved maps have tables of the conventions adopted, and here again a historical study of some interest is possible.

But, for the practical student, and the teacher, it is sufficient for my purpose to direct attention again to the sixpenny book issued by the Ordnance Survey, the shilling army study of map-reading, and particularly to the table of explanations found at the foot of every sheet of the international map.

Perhaps I ought to remind the reader again, in connection with this subject, that nothing on a map, beyond the distance of determinate points, is in accord with any scale, except in the case of very large-scale plans, such as the 25″ ordnance map in this country. Individual drawings on a map are all *pictorial* representations of the objects to which they direct attention; rivers and roads are drawn on the line of direction, often many hundred times wider than they would be if they could be drawn and distinguished by the eye on the true scale of the map. I refer to this point again, as it is of great importance that it should be fully appreciated by the teacher.

Of course, in the choice of elements of graphic expression in relation to the pictorial features of maps there has been a gradual elimination of unsuitable signs, and the "survival of the fittest" has produced a stereotyped uniformity—very essential in cartography, now an exact and highly-developed science. Thus, for the student of this science, as for the working cartographer, the whole matter presents itself in a satisfactory and simple form, even in that of the conventional *size* of pictorial objects as suitable for delineation on maps of different scales.

It is usual to superimpose geological colouring upon a map of which the details are already engraved. This arrangement has, to a certain extent, the effect of degrading and obscuring these details, but it is usually practised, mainly on the grounds of economy, in map production.

No one can be even a student of geography without recognizing the dependence of that science upon geology. No one can look with intelligence on any portion of the earth's surface without feeling the need of some knowledge of the underlying rock formations, in order to obtain a real understanding of what is before him. Every feature of such surface depends for its form and character upon stratigraphical geology—mountain ranges, hills and plains, the course of rivers and even of roads, are based upon the underlying rocks, their texture, and their slope and relative positions. In these circumstances geological maps are essential to geographical teaching.

The coloration of such maps, the distinctions in sequences of time and in material and character as depicted on maps are now reduced to a settled system, and no study of cartography, even in its simplest form, can be really useful unless these conventions are followed and understood. Apart from colouring, the most important technical indications on a geological map are those of the "faults," or dislocations of the continuity of the rocks they affect. They determine in a large, and sometimes in a dominant measure the configuration of the surface, and should therefore be carefully studied. Faults are usually shown on the coloured ground by white lines.

One other branch of the subject of geographical expression has much actuality, as connected with the world-war. In military cartography all details non-essential to the immediate military object are, as far as possible, eliminated (as, for instance, historical and archaeological details which are of interest to the general cartographer), and special prominence is given to the position and character of all objects on a map which have military utility, either for defensive or offensive purposes, as points of observation, as means of communication, or of concealment. Special nomenclature and special conventional forms are adopted, and everything is reduced to its simplest expression. As a soldier, in examining a landscape before him with a view to the most rapid and efficient development of rifle, machine-gun, or artillery fire, classifies all objects, and sees, for example, but three kinds of trees, the bushy-topped tree, the fir-tree and the poplar, so, on the map, a church is a building which has, or has not, for him a tower, and in addition may, or may not, have a spire. To the civilian a church, on a map, is a church and nothing else; to the soldier it is a point of observation, or defence, or a distinctive object on which, or by which, to direct or control fire, or to direct a line of advance or retreat. These are examples. They illustrate the essential and special ideas which dominate military cartography and map-reading. Their study seems to me valuable in clearing the mind of the teacher in dealing with maps generally.

Maps of entrenched and stabilized fronts, as drawn in the Great War from aerial observation, are works of great beauty and technical skill. The cutting up—as was practised—of large areas of country into accurately plotted squares and quarter-squares, lettered and numbered, so as to enable the entrenched line to direct infallibly artillery fire to exact points from batteries far in the rear, was a triumph of practical cartography and a development of the highest military importance.

I have already drawn attention to the possibility of co-ordinating panoramic views with maps, and of using this association of different elements of the same subject in an illustrative and instructional sense. I venture to again commend these ideas to the teacher even if it is not always possible to develop them largely in practice for want of suitable material.

Globes are a special form of cartographic art. They are of great antiquity; but very few early specimens have survived.

In modern times there has been a great output of terrestrial as well as of celestial globes, mainly for instructional purposes. Their value in this sense lies in the realization by the pupil of the spherical form of the earth, and of the relation of the main areas of land surface to the larger part covered by the sea. Globes cannot, in general, be made large enough to have much interest from the point of view of the details of surface. In the eighteenth century globes were manufactured in large numbers in this country, and sold at high prices. A firm of globe-makers now carrying on business advertise their manufacture as having commenced as far back as 1702. John Cary, who has been already referred to, was associated with his brother William, the astronomical instrument-maker, in the production of globes. They carried on business in the Strand in adjoining houses, Nos. 181 and 182, until January 17th, 1820, when they were both burnt out, and John Cary removed to St James's Street. The catalogues they issued, which are found, commonly, at the end of John Cary's itineraries, atlases and other publications, show that a considerable business was carried on. There were other globe-makers then, as there are now, but large globes are not, I think, much used at the present time.

Very large globes have been built, and in those cases the mapping details have usually been painted on the interior.

The international map, as has already been mentioned, is arranged with the sheets in gores, so that, when it is completed, they will form a globe one-millionth of the earth's actual size, or about 42 feet in diameter.

No school, of course, should be without globes, whatever its outfit in maps may be.

PART II

XIII

SUMMARY.

(*a*) History.

It will be remembered that the period of the production of maps is here divided on the same lines as one adopts for the historical classification of books, that is to say, into the period before the invention of the arts of printing and engraving, during which the preparation of maps and charts was the work of the individual, and the multiplication of copies (if it was attempted) was the laborious occupation of the manual copyist, and the subsequent period of constant multiplication from engraved plates and type.

Roughly speaking, the year 1500 is a convenient point of time for the division of these periods.

As has been noticed, however, the first collection, in engraved form, of a series of maps, is the *Theatrum Orbis Terrarum* of Abraham Ortelius, published at Antwerp in 1570, and this is really the date from which one can start in regard to the systematic multiplication of maps for sale, recognising the previous seventy or eighty years as a period of tentative effort and of individual experiment in engraved cartography, equivalent to the period of the so-called *incunabula* as applied to the historical classification of printed books.

We have thus a modern period of about 350 years of prolific production of engraved maps, from 1570 to 1920, which is easy to bear in mind.

The historical development of geographical knowledge, as translated and recorded in maps, is rather more complex, and is subject to more than one element of classification. The early scientific studies of the earth's form and surface, recorded from about 500 years before the Christian era, were limited in their results not so much by the conceptions of the learned of those times (which one may consider very advanced) as by the extremely imperfect character of their instruments of precision and of their personal means of travel, movement, and the communication of facts.

This period of something like 700 years ends with Claudius Ptolemaeus (Ptolemy) and his *Geographia*.

During the dominance of the Roman imperial system, cartography practically ceased to exist, as far as our knowledge goes, as a general science, and there is thus almost an historical blank, separating the early scientific period from that of our modern developments.

Ptolemy should therefore be fixed in the mind, not as a single and unique exponent of the geographical knowledge of the seven hundred years of research which laid the foundation of his work, or because his conclusions were extraordinary for their accuracy, but because he stands as a landmark at the close of a well-defined period.

From his time a period of at least 1200 years must be regarded as a desert for the historian of cartography, except for the commencement, towards the end of the period, of the accurate coastal surveys of the Mediterranean pilots.

Some land-maps were indeed drawn towards the end of this period in Europe, but their cartographic value is very small, and the geographical knowledge displayed very indifferent.

It was in 1409 that Ptolemy's *Geographia* became known in Central Europe by a Latin translation, but it was not until 1475 that a version of his text appeared in print.

Maps drawn on Ptolemy's data began to appear three years later, in 1478, and the period known as that of the revival of Ptolemy commenced, and, with it, the revival of cartography as a science.

But it must be borne in mind that a servile respect for the learning of Ptolemy, as displayed in his *Geographia*, obscured the serious errors he adopted and perpetuated, and that this deference to the Ptolemaic tradition vitiated cartographic conclusions for a considerable length of time.

Parallel with these developments, the actual coastal surveys carried on by mariners in the Mediterranean and extended to the Atlantic coasts, were being embodied in the comparatively accurate portolan charts, of which the period is, roughly, as far as they are known from existing specimens, about 1300 to 1550, or 250 years.

The Ptolemaic foundation and the practical work of navigators were equally absorbed into the new cartography, when the discovery of the New World, the extension of sea voyages, the growth of the adventurous spirit and of commercial enterprise, combined with the new means of representation of surface by designs on engraved plates, laid a foundation on which was built the map-work of the prolific Dutch and Flemish School—from 1570 and for a century onwards—from which development flowed the great cartographic stream of production of which we now survey the results.

This modern period is easily divisible into that of empirical methods, approaching slowly by the painful accumulation of details to comparative accuracy, and that of the modern system of fixing points accurately by triangulation.

As triangulation has its earliest systematic application in France, we can record the year 1744 as marking the commencement of this scientific accuracy as adapted to map construction.

Questions of scale, orientation and meridian, though of interest in themselves, do not sufficiently dominate cartographic progress to invite classification of maps in time upon these bases alone.

In tabular form, the classification I recommend to the teacher is thus shaped (see Table, p. 59).

(*b*) Art.

The review of the art of map-drawing, which has already been given in a rather sketchy and incomplete manner, cannot be usefully condensed further.

This subject is so much a visual one that it can only be followed up with any success through an inspection and careful comparative study of typical examples.

It is an unfortunate fact that nowhere in any public institution, as far as I am aware, has any attempt been made to group together an illustrative exhibition of maps in historical sequence. Such an exhibition, as an aid to study and especially to teaching, would be of the greatest value. The British Museum has all the material for such display, but the authorities of that great national storehouse of knowledge have never up to now recognized the possibilities in this direction.

(*c*) Technical Characteristics.

The extensive study which is possible of the technical characteristics of maps can be best summarised in the form adopted in my syllabus (pp. 75—80 *post*).

It is of course important to classify in the mind the three fundamental ideas (i) of *size* relative to the portion of the surface of the world represented on the map, which is translated in the *scale*; (ii) of the position of the various points

Period	Graphic method employed	Classification of Map-periods	Association with Nationalities	Nature of cartographic production	Dates	Approx. period in yrs.
I	Hand-drawn	Ancient scientific study of the earth and its surface, as far as then known	Babylonians, Egyptians, Greeks	Few, or no, actual maps	500 B.C. to Ptolemy (second century A.D.)	700
II	Hand-drawn	Interval of decay in geographical knowledge and its application to cartography	Roman Empire and early Middle Ages (Europe)	Very few maps; mainly road-maps	Second to fifteenth centuries	1200
III	Engraved	Revival of Ptolemy	Middle Ages (Europe)	Maps drawn on the basis of the *Geographia* (Ptolemy)	Fifteenth and sixteenth centuries	150
IV	Engraved	Modern cartography	Dutch, French, English and other European schools. World cartography	(*a*) Maps drawn on empirical methods, increasing in practical accuracy	Sixteenth and seventeenth centuries (1500 to 1700)	200
				(*b*) Triangulation and exact cartography	Eighteenth and nineteenth centuries (1700 to 1920)	200

Portolan charts 1300 to 1550 (250 years)

on the map in relation to one another in *direction*, to which *orientation* is applied; and (iii) of fixing the *position* of the area delineated on the surface of the earth, determined by the use of conventional lines of longitude and latitude, or *meridian* lines.

It is necessary to study carefully the gradual evolution of technical method in cartographic expression which, through the survival of the fittest, has produced a series of well-settled and familiar conventions. And it is desirable to reinforce the knowledge of these matters and of their application by some realization of the relations of views and panoramas to maps, and of the character and construction of maps in actual relief, and by what was formerly called "the use of the globes."

These facts and ideas must be clearly associated in the mind of the teacher, if he is to give a living interest to his lessons, and is to create an interest in maps and all that surrounds them amongst his pupils.

PART III

XIV

TEACHING: PRACTICAL SUGGESTIONS.

IN this section an endeavour is made to apply to the art of teaching, in class, of geography and cartography, with special reference to the latter subject, the information conveyed and classified in the preceding pages, in which it is hoped that the reader may have already gathered some hints of practical value.

I am here merely putting together, in a purely suggestive form, what it appears to me may be usefully considered in relation to the practical work of teachers, more particularly in elementary schools.

It is obvious that, to obtain success in the transmission of knowledge, there must be personal sympathy in the relations between the teacher and his class.

Further, there must be such acquaintance with the subject of instruction in the teacher as may enable him to attain to simplicity of form and substance and to a direct and attractive character in the illustrations he employs. In such a practical matter as geography simplicity of ideas is of the first importance, and this is only to be obtained through a real appreciation of the value and importance of the subject to be taught. This appreciation at its true value may be derived, very largely, from the historical side of the questions involved; from a knowledge of the outlines, at least, of the growth, parallel to the development of general information and civilisation, of geography and its application to map-making.

A broad view of the gradual development of human effort in these directions should establish in the mind of the teacher a natural and effective interest in his subject, and should advance his outlook far beyond the mere questions of geographical limits as laid down on maps, and the enumeration and classification of centres of population, means of communication, and variations of character in the surface of the earth, matters with which the teacher is too often content.

It has thus been a dominant object of this treatise to establish the outlines, at least in an adequate form, of historical sequence and development as applied to maps.

The second point at which a teacher should aim is that of obtaining a clear and practical conception of the map itself, as a record, in a conventional form, of facts, and as a means of instruction.

Here again simplicity is of the first importance. It may be interesting to obtain some knowledge of the growth of convention, but, in practice, the teacher may well content himself with a careful study of the methods of expression in actual use in cartography as they are now stereotyped. The historical side of this subject has no special value in ordinary teaching.

My proposition in substance is this: That the teacher, in self-preparation for his professional task in this department of knowledge, should found on these two branches of the subject—(i) the history of geographical progress in its application to maps and map-making, and (ii) the character and meaning of the technical materials of which a map is composed.

This is a very broad and generalized expression of the

objects to be attained by the diligent, sympathetic and intelligent teacher in his own training.

With regard to teaching to which I now pass, there are two branches of the subject and its application which should be kept distinct. They are the study of the technical form which experience and convention has established for the map, and of the surface of the earth, and the translation in pictorial representation of that surface to the map. The latter subject is, of course, of immense variety and interest, and of the highest educational value—the former may perhaps be regarded as in the main mechanical.

It will be noticed that while as regards the training of the teacher himself I consider the history of maps as of importance, I do not suggest that this foundation of general knowledge can, in ordinary schools, be imported into class instruction, except as a useful illustrative feature. Time would probably not here be available for such instruction whatever might be possible in schools of a higher class.

As, before you draw a picture, or sit down to write a book, you must, in the first case, learn how to use your pencil and your brush, and study colours and the way they should be mixed and put on paper or canvas, and, in the second, must practise the formation of letters and words on paper with the pen, must study the alphabet, the words made up from letters and the sentences from words, must understand the conventional system of punctuation, so that proper pause and emphasis may be given to sentences when read, and the arrangements of sentences and phrases in paragraphs and chapters, must, in a word, be familiar with the mechanism of the art, so you should I think, before you embark on map construction, before you endeavour to translate the facts of geography, of your actual examination of the world and its surface, study the conventions, the technical methods of cartography and of the map itself.

This subject, when examined, presents much interest, and may, in skilful hands, have an illuminating influence in teaching even on the rather inadequate basis of the ordinary flat map.

Being then supplied with the basis of technical knowledge as applied to maps and their construction, the teacher is armed for the effort to attack geography as a science.

I have endeavoured to emphasize the main points to be always kept in view—those essential to the map and to geography—direction, proportion and location. I need not amplify them further. They are obviously the absolute essentials of cartographic expression. The pictorial character of the ordinary map must also be thoroughly grasped, and the imagination must be adequately trained to this conception.

The fixing of points by triangulation must also be borne in mind as the constructive basis of modern maps.

In the classification of the general subject for the purpose of instruction, I venture to suggest, in accordance with the views I have already expressed, progression in the following order:

In the main it is an endeavour to train the mind of the child by founding on the known and the simple in order to gradually advance into the region of the unknown and the complex, which is, of course, the natural line of the development of knowledge.

The idea is to study in the first instance map-drawing, and the use of maps, and map-reading, as distinguished from the study of geography itself, or of the facts of which maps are the pictorial record. This is the study of the map as a pictorial expression drawn on highly technical lines.

It is probable that in the ordinary elementary school the usual course of training in map-drawing and in geography, as taught in text-books, will be followed in the earlier stages, and that the method I here suggest will be applied later—in classes of which the general instruction is somewhat advanced. I offer no opinion on the standard to be attained before departing from the approved routine, and, indeed, there is no antagonism between the two methods of education, and they may be usefully pursued simultaneously on parallel lines.

I suggest that, at such a stage as may be found convenient, a class should be instructed somewhat in the following manner.

The teacher, using the blackboard, or a large sheet of paper, preferably ruled up into squares of some definite size, or scale, should proceed to construct a map, drawing, as largely as possible, upon the knowledge of his class of the actual locality of the school itself. This is, naturally, a method more easily adapted to the village with its open spaces and its many familiar and representative characteristics, than to a town area with its rigid outlines of streets, and its want of originality and local character.

Probably the first point to consider (and in the whole of this class of teaching the mind of the child should be drawn upon by interrogation and suggestion, and every effort should be made to cultivate his imaginative and constructive faculties, so that the map to be drawn, however crude or distorted it may be, is rather the work of the class than of the teacher) is that of direction.

The question of what standard of direction to fix, and the well-settled system of placing the map with the north at the top, should be discussed, and the class should accept, with knowledge, the meaning of this fundamental basis of the map.

This might be followed up by fixing on the blackboard or paper, by a line radiating from the school, or the church, or some other recognized centre, the direction of some well-known object. Other directions might similarly be fixed, to the number of a dozen perhaps, or such as may be convenient having regard to the knowledge which the class possesses of the immediate neighbourhood.

The map, at this stage, would show a central point, some radiating lines of direction, and indications of the cardinal points of the compass.

Having thoroughly established the idea of direction, the next practical point to be worked out would be that of distance, and the class must, before the distances of the objects agreed to be recorded on the map can be represented, attain to the conception of scale or proportion. If miles are being dealt with they should be translated into inches on the map, or, if the scale is a large one, as would probably be the case, miles might be translated on the map into feet.

Whatever distances are assigned, by the common consent of the class, to the objects selected, as from the agreed centre, these should be marked off on the scale selected. It would then be well to use the scale to establish the distance between some of the objects, thus obtaining the idea of triangulation, and the constructive development of the map as a whole.

I think it unnecessary to deal with the more general question of the location of the map under construction upon the surface of the earth, though, of course, at some stage of instruction this matter might be introduced by reference to a large map of the county or district and to the position of the embryonic map as defined by meridian lines.

Having obtained the skeleton of the map, drawn exclusively from the knowledge and intelligence of the class, it becomes necessary to give it some pictorial character, and here the imagination of the class can be drawn upon with the ultimate aid of the conventions of ordinary mapping.

Details of pictorial representation of the objects of which the points are now fixed, and of others in relative positions, should be gradually worked-in on the surface of the map, and the whole question of the use of such methods thoroughly investigated and discussed. The child's mind, and that of the teacher also, may be usefully exercised in many directions in the search for convenient forms of expression, although ultimately the conventions of ordinary mapping will be adhered to. In the hands of the intelligent teacher much may be learned and much may be taught both of direct and collateral interest and value. The ordinary features of maps may be drawn-in and explained.

No doubt a first effort may lead to results of not much cartographic value, but the object I imagine in this form of educational exercise is to be found in ideas and methods of expression rather than in their results.

It is unnecessary for me to elaborate in great detail the development of teaching on these lines. They are suggestive and admit of amplification in a very large measure. What I urge especially is that the constructive effort should be imposed on the class and should not come from the teacher, and that the children should draw upon their own knowledge, memory, and even imagination.

The elementary conception of the map and of its construction thus obtained must be used to illuminate all work on maps and the study of the globe.

At a more advanced stage, the flow of water in rivers, the size, character and direction of roads and of railways, the slope and elevation of hills and mountains, the character of surface—woods, cultivated ground, marshes—and all other details of a general character can be studied, in relation to their representation on maps.

Without laying down any rule as to the method, or extent, by which such instruction should be developed or limited, but leaving much to the teacher, to the time at his disposal, and to the intelligence both of the teacher and the taught, I pass on to the second stage of instruction which I suggest should be followed—that of the actual examination of some portion of the earth's surface and the construction of a map on the method already reached as a result of such practical study.

Here again direction is the first point for consideration, and in practice this is so obvious that it has probably, in the ordinary person, never received any consideration at all.

One of the objects to be attained, in the first instance, is the training of the individual in the habit of observation. The military training of the soldier is an example of method. This training begins in the barrack yard, where the recruit is made to count the number of windows, the number of trees, and to observe the size of objects and their relative positions; his training continues in the open country, and he is gradually educated so as to become an expert observer of natural and artificial features in a landscape, and acutely alive to every feature of military importance. In civil life this form of practical training is generally ignored, and the individual suffers accordingly in his physical capacity.

In the geographical training on the practical side something may be incidentally gained in habits of general value. I suggest therefore that the school playground should be—as is the barrack square—the elementary ground for study both of direction, in the geographical sense, and of the habit of observation and of recording in the memory, or on paper, the other external aspects of the world.

The use of the sun and of the stars for determining direction, with a view to movement on the earth's surface, or to the drawing of maps, may well be studied in the playground, or on the village green.

The comparison between what has already been learnt of the method of conventional map-drawing can there be discussed, and the classification of objects in accordance with the conventions adopted can be followed up.

The position of the school site relative to the points of the compass should be established, and the compass itself should be used and the variations between the true and magnetic north explained.

Map construction on the surface of the playground itself on a scale agreed might be attempted, and directions laid out with the compass, and distances measured with a tape might help to carry on, from the small-scale map of the school-room, the natural sequence of ideas towards the outer world.

Whatever this stage might produce (and it opens a large field for ingenuity and the exercise of the teacher's art), the further progress I suggest is that of actual examination of country.

The class will readily understand the need of direction when it proceeds along a road, footpath, or street, or across an open space. The children might be taken for a certain distance and then be questioned on the direction in which they had moved, and might further endeavour to establish the distance itself. They should obtain comparative ideas of distance in relation to the space between telegraph or telephone posts, lamp posts, trees, and by noting the size of buildings, and even the appearance of objects of known dimensions at various distances from the observer, following the lines of "judging distance" as practised in the army. In the result, something in the nature of an outline map of the road followed could be prepared, with marginal notes, supplementary to pictorial details, the whole combining the various typical characteristics of the ordinary map.

Habits of observation and of record of numerical details and of the characteristics of objects to be noted on the map could be further cultivated. Such particulars as the direction of flow of water in streams might usefully lead to an attempt to realize the various channels through which the water reaches the sea and the point of entrance. Water-sheds and water-partings would thus come naturally under discussion and the relations of centres of populations to rivers and many other questions might be incidentally dealt with. The range of interest in the natural and artificial surroundings of human life has no limit.

The discussion of direction might be based on the position of the sun at various periods of the day; similarly the stars could be utilised in the early evenings in winter.

As to distance, measurement with a tape or chain might be employed, the number of paces might be counted, or relative calculations based on objects at known and fixed intervals be made. Time might also be used, by marching a fixed distance in a certain time as recorded and using movement at the same rate of march as a standard.

Observations as to the height of trees and of houses might be made directly, and, in convenient circumstances, calculations might be based on the length of shadows.

The results of expeditions of this character outside the school grounds might be worked up into map form in the school-room, either from memory, or notes, or by using both foundations.

More ambitious schemes might be developed under favourable conditions, and elementary surveying, with the chain and cross-staff, carried on at a distance from the school.

The recent suggestions for regional surveys adapt themselves to these methods of practical training, and represent a further development of observation and record, incorporating historical and archaeological investigations and study, and the recording of the results obtained in cartographic form. The time taken up by such investigations can hardly, however, be regarded as available within the limits of a school time-table, and regional surveys must, I think, be generally relegated to half-holidays, or other spare time, if they are to achieve anything beyond the most perfunctory results.

So much is now known of the history and archaeology of this country that, although in an educational sense the system of regional survey is interesting, and has no doubt considerable value, the additions to knowledge likely to be obtained must be regarded as small and unimportant. Nevertheless, the knowledge of one's own district distributed throughout the population by means of such surveys, associated with the local school as a centre, cannot but be most valuable in the advance of general education. The system recommended falls in very well with my ideas of practical instruction in cartography as here outlined, and I should much like to see it adopted generally throughout the country.

These practical methods of study lead to a more general conception of the value and character of maps than is probably obtainable through the routine class teaching from hand-books now uniformly pursued. They will in their results merge into the latter and enable teacher and student to realize better than would, on the average, be otherwise the case what is aimed at in map construction.

It would be desirable in the higher standards of a school to carry further the ideas of technical expression from the point now reached on the dual road of geographical study.

The question of scale in particular, probably often a subject of confusion in the realization of size and distance, requires simple treatment and explanation on the lines I have already indicated.

The best foundation to start from is, of course, the globe, which co-ordinates all proportions on the earth's surface, and from this point of view the international (or World) map on the scale of one-millionth seems to me the most valuable educational material we possess. One, at least, of its sheets should be part of the outfit of every school in which there is any pretence to teaching geography.

Similarly the Ordnance Survey maps should be utilized.

For any regional survey, and for any proper adaptation of the empirical method or actual perambulation of a district with a view to the educational construction of maps which I have advocated above, sheets of the 6″ and of the 25″ maps should be available. Unfortunately the cost of a series of sheets of both maps prepared and suitably mounted to form a map of an area of sufficient size with the school buildings as a centre, which I should like to see in every elementary school, is considerable.

The ideal would be to have the three ordnance maps: 25″, 6″, and 1″ cut to the same square of about 4 ft × 4 ft, with the school as a centre marked by a flag, and with coloured circles at 1 mile intervals drawn on each from this centre. Such a series of maps would show, in a specially graphic form, the difference of scale, and could be used, in teaching, to illustrate the relations of various scales as applied to a given surface.

Another method would be, on the basis of 25″ sheets cut

to a 4 ft square, to frame a map with insets of 6″ sheets and 1″ sheets of the same area about 1 foot and 2 inches square respectively. The same comparisons and illustrations would result, but not I think in quite the best form. The expense would, of course, be less in this case than in the more ambitious scheme.

The educational outfit of every school should include a fair-sized geological map of England and Wales and some local sheets of the 1″ geological survey maps. It should also include the Index Ordnance maps of the county showing the parishes and the areas of the urban and rural districts and boroughs. Some maps showing elevations above mean sea-level, climatic zones, and other regional details should also be in every school, but to what extent this could be carried out by a selection amongst the many valuable maps already in existence depends in practice on the question of expense.

Finally I return to the History of Maps which may be regarded as a part of education more advanced than the instruction which can be given in an elementary school. It is partially a question of general history, and should be perhaps associated with historical teaching.

The history of cartography; the art applied to the production of maps; the various special developments of map subjects, and the whole of the large group of their technical details, present together a magnificent field of instructional activity, illustrative of geography, of history itself, and of art and technical skill.

As regards method in education as applied to these aspects of the science, no special rules can be usefully laid down. The syllabus issued in anticipation of the lectures upon which the foregoing is based gives in a sufficiently convenient form the headings and indications of sequence which may be followed (page 75 *post*).

An amplification of these subjects in detail can be worked up to almost any extent beyond the limits here set, by drawing upon text-books and upon articles in encyclopædias and other similar works.

For any really successful exploration of this large field a considerable collection of representative specimens of maps illustrative of cartographical progress and of the art of technical detail must be regarded as essential. As has already been noticed no such collection is, however, generally available, and there is thus a practical difficulty in giving adequate illustrative support to what is, if simply an enumeration of the names of map-makers and of the dates of their publications, with a technical outline of their work and productivity in chronological order, a very arid narrative.

Something might be done by careful selection and the publication of a series of representative specimens, to put the teaching of historical geography on a better footing, and to give adequate expression to cartography in its historical aspects; but much care and a large expenditure would be necessary to obtain satisfactory results.

The table found on page 59 *ante* is an attempt to classify, in a rather general form, the results of cartographical progress from the earliest times to the present. It can be used as a foundation for teaching, and, with the syllabus, supplies probably a sufficient outline upon which to base the instructional study of the whole subject.

APPENDIX

MAPS: THEIR HISTORY, CHARACTERISTICS AND USES

(With Special Reference to Teaching)

Syllabus of the Lectures as originally delivered

INTRODUCTION.

LIMITS AND OBJECTS OF THE CARTOGRAPHER: Plane Surface; Elevation; Flow of Water; Means of Travel and Communication (Road-Maps); Special Feature (Geological, etc.).

CHARACTERISTICS OF MAPS AND CHARTS: Pictorial and Scriptorial; Art and Decoration; Simplicity an essential feature; Difficulty of its combination with detail; Coloration; Reproduction by Engraving and Printing.

CARTOGRAPHICAL ELEMENTS: Scale (proportion); Orientation (direction); Meridian, longitude and latitude (location); Technical and Conventional Methods of Expression (contours, layers, hachures, use of colours and shadings, etc.).

TERMINOLOGY: *Theatrum* (Ortelius, 1570); Atlas (Mercator, 1595); *Typus*; *Tabula*; Map; Chart; *Portolano*, etc.

HISTORY.

PERIODS: (*a*) Production of individual maps.
(*b*) Reproduction in quantity by Engraving and Printing.

HISTORICAL PROGRESS:

Egyptians.

Babylonians (division of arc of Meridian into 360°, 60′ and 60″).

Greeks (Posidonius, *circa* 130–50 B.C.; Claudius Ptolemaeus, second century A.D.).

Romans (*Tabula Peutingeriana*, third century).

Arabians (Mariner's Compass).

Portolan Charts of the Mediterranean Sea, etc. Voyage of St Louis (1270); first signed example now known, 1311.

Revival of Ptolemy—discovery of his *Geographia*, fifteenth century; his errors of measurement founded on Posidonius, making the Mediterranean one-third too long; corrected by de Lisle in 1700.

First engraved map (wood-block), 1460; *Theatrum Orbis Terrarum* (Abraham Ortelius, Antwerp, 1570); Saxton's Maps of the English Counties, 1579; Bouguereau's *Théâtre François*, 1594; Jean Le Clerc, 1619, etc.

The German and Italian Schools (sixteenth century).

The Dutch and Flemish School (sixteenth and seventeenth centuries). Ortelius, Mercator, the Hondius, Jansons and Blaeus.

The French School (seventeenth and eighteenth centuries). Sanson of Abbeville (1600–1667) and his sons, Nicholas, Adrien and Guillaume, and their co-workers and successors the Jaillots and Robert de Vaugondys (1658–1757), and others.

The English School (seventeenth and eighteenth centuries). Christopher Saxton (1579); John Norden (1593); John Speed (1610); John Ogilby (road-maps) (1675); Seller (1676); Morden, Moll and Senex; Thomas and Emanuel Bowen and Thomas Kitchin (1760); Cary and Arrowsmith (1783 and 1790).

Period of Exact and Modern Cartography, based on Triangulation; France (Cassini, 1744); England (Ordnance Survey, commenced 1783, first sheet of 1-inch map published 1 January 1801).

Modern Cartography (nineteenth and twentieth centuries). Map production from aerial photographs.

Geological Maps. Wm Smith (1815–24); Geological Coast-Line Sections (Phillips and Mantell); Marine Coast-Line Drawings (Drake's last voyage, 1595).

Sea-Charts; Hydrographical Surveys and Soundings.

ART.

Hand-painted; Mosaic Pavements; Tapestry; Needlework.

Engraving; Wood-block, Road-Map of Germany, 1501; of Italy, Toussains Denis, 1515.

Copperplate; Saxton, Speed, etc.

Lithography.

Colour Printing (nineteenth century).

Photo-zincography.

Portolan Charts—their decoration.

Illumination, French School (seventeenth century).

Decorative details; Dutch, English, French (Nicolas Sanson and his engravers—Cordier, Peyrounin, etc.); The Atlas of the Jaillots (1696); *l'Atlas Universel* (Robert de Vaugondy, 1757).

Italian Maps (Rizzi-Zannoni, 1793 and 1794).

Modern Maps—without adventitious ornament. English, French and Swiss; World-Map on the scale of one-millionth in 2084 sheets.

VARIOUS AND SPECIAL MAPS.

EARLIEST OBJECTS: Travel; War; Commerce; Road-Maps; Sea-Maps.

SPECIAL OBJECTS OF CARTOGRAPHICAL REPRESENTATION: Military, attack and defence; Plans of Fortresses and Sieges; Records of the movements of Armies and Fleets; National and other Boundaries; Climatic, Racial and Geological Conditions; Winds and Currents; Panoramas —mixed plan and profile.

TECHNICAL CHARACTERISTICS.

SCALE: Its historical development; English method, "inch to a mile"; fractional method, *e.g.* $\frac{1}{25000}$; Variety and Uniformity of Scale; French map of 1751; International Map, Scale $\frac{1}{1000000}$.

MERIDIAN: Its history; Degrees of latitude and longitude; the Babylonians; Posidonius; Ptolemy; Modern Calculations.

ORIENTATION: Purely conventional. Roman maps generally South at the top; so also Arabian maps. Early Mediaeval maps East at the top, and, in border, a representation of Paradise; on Maps of eighteenth century East still distinguished specially by a cross; Portolan Charts North at top (dependent on compass). Magnetic and true North; Variations of compass.

HISTORY OF INITIAL MERIDIAN: Ptolemy—Azores, or Canary Islands—used by cartographers up to end of seventeenth century, and by the French up to the Revolution of 1789. In England—London from 1676 (Seller) and later St Paul's; Greenwich Observatory (founded in 1675) from 1794 (John Cary). Earlier London is 20° 30′ East (Francis Lamb, 1669).

EXPRESSION OF SURFACE: Mountains; Plains (hachures, contours, layers); Depth of Water; Rivers; Canals; Roads; Railroads; Telegraph Wires; Coloration and Shading (woods, forests, meadows, marshes, sand, ice, etc.); Towns and Villages (population and area); Churches; Monastic Buildings; Post and Telegraph Offices, etc.

QUESTIONS OF DETAIL AND DIVERSITY: Size of objects as drawn on maps.

GEOLOGICAL COLOURING SUPERIMPOSED: Geological "faults."

MILITARY DETAILS—elimination of all non-essential elements, and historical particulars; maps of defensive positions.

PANORAMIC ASPECTS OF CARTOGRAPHY apply only with success to well-marked features, such as mountain ranges and coast lines.

MAPS IN ACTUAL RELIEF: Vertical and horizontal scales.

GLOBES: Their history and uses.

RÉSUMÉ.

TEACHING.

To build up from the particular to the general.

To found upon a real knowledge of the objects of cartography.

To give some idea of its historical development.

To treat with simplicity the technical details and their meaning.

To cultivate the habit of comparative observation.

To avoid excessive memorization and endeavour to create a realistic and an imaginative sense.

To use the intelligence of the pupils by giving them a concrete object of distance or direction, or of characteristics of the local situation.

To study orientation by the stars, by the sun, and by the use of prevailing winds.

To study a road on foot, noticing, with the compass in hand, its changes of direction, its character, its bridges, and the houses on either side, for example.

Then to draw a map upon that basis, and test the impressions and ideas conveyed, both by question and answer, and by reference to a large-scale Ordnance Map.

Generally to treat the map as a book from which to learn —not as a final object of study in itself.

INDEX

Adams, Robert, 32
Africa, coast-lines of, 12, 13
America, coast-lines of, 13
American Continent, discovery of, 10, 57
d'Anville, Jean Baptiste Bourguignon (1697–1782), 17
Arrowsmith, Aaron (1750–1823), 17
Arte of Navigation, The, 43
Atlantic coasts, 12, 13, 37, 57
Atlas Anglicanus, 4
Atlas (*Cary's New and Correct English Atlas*), 45
Atlas Géographique et Militaire de la France, 17, 27, 38, 41
Atlas Manuale, 44
Atlas Nouveau, contenant toutes les Parties du Monde, 23
Atlas Siegfried, 47
Atlas Universel, 17
Auvergne, map of, 31, 34
Azores, meridian of, 42, 43, 44, 45

Berey, Nicolas, 23
Bibliotheca Topographica Anglicana, 15
Blaeu family, the, 13, 26, 44
Blome, Richard (d. 1705), 45
Boisseau, Jean (*fl.* 1636–51), 7, 14, 23
Bouguereau, Maurice, 7
Bowen, Emanuel, 4, 17
Bowen, Thomas (d. 1790), 4, 17
Brazils, coast-line of the, 12
Britannia (Blome), 45
Britannia (Camden), 16, 43
Britannia (Ogilby), 16
British cartographers, 14, 15, 16, 17
British Isles, maps of, 14, 15, 45
Buache, Philippe, 47

Cambridge Antiquarian Society, *Communications* of the, 19
Cambridgeshire maps, catalogue of, 19
Camden, William (1551–1623), 16, 43
Canary Islands, meridian of, 42, 44, 45
Cape Verde Islands, meridian of, 44
Capitaine, Louis, 18, 27
Carte Dufour, 48
Carte Géometrique de la France, 18
Cartes Générales de Toutes les Parties du Monde, 4
Cary, G. and J., 19
Cary, John (1754–1835), 17, 19, 27, 45, 54
Cary, William (1759–1825), 54
Cassini de Thury, César François (1714–84), 18
Cassini de Thury, Jacques Dominique (1748–1845), 18
Catalan navigators, 12, 41
Central Europe, route-map of, 25, 37
Columbus, Christopher (*c.* 1436–1506), 10, 11
Cordier, R., 26
Cortes, Martin, 42
Corvo, meridian of, 44
County of Cambridge, maps of, 19

Davis, John, 43, 44
Drake, Sir Francis (*c.* 1545–95), 20
Dutch cartographers, 13, 23, 26, 47, 48, 49, 57

England and Wales, maps of, 14, 15, 16, 17

English counties, maps of, 4, 15, 16
Eratosthenes of Cyrene (276–196 B.C.), 10
Etzlaub, Erhard, 25
Europe, coast-lines of, 12

Faden, William, 17 *n.*
Ferro, meridian of, 44, 45
Flemish cartographers, 14, 57
Forteventura, meridian of, 44
Fortresses, plans of, 32, 33
France, maps of, 26, 27, 38, 41
— triangulation of, 18, 57
French cartographers, 14, 17, 18, 48, 49
Fuego, Isla del, meridian of, 44

Galle, Philippe (1537–1612), 13 *n.*
Galliae tabule geographicae, 8
Gallic *leuga*, 16
Gassendi, Pierre (1592–1655), 44
Geographia (Ptolemy), 11, 56, 57, 59
Germany, road-map of, 25, 30
Great Level of the Fens, maps of, 19
Green, William, 42
Greenwich, meridian of, 42, 45
Greenwood, C. and J., 28, 28 *n.*

Hecataeus of Miletus (*c.* 550–475 B.C.), 10
History of the Drainage of the Great Level of the Fens, 19
Hole, William (*fl.* 1600–30), 16
Holland, Philemon (1552–1637), 43
Hondius family, the, 13

Indicateur Fidèle, 33
International (or World) map, 18, 39, 40, 42, 45, 54, 72
Isle de France, map of, 4, 31
Isle de Rhé, map of, 31
Italian navigators, 12, 41
Italy, map of, 25

Jaillot family, the, 5, 14, 23, 26, 35
Janson family, the, 13, 44
Jode, Gerard de (1515–91), 8
John Cary, Engraver, Map, Chart and Print-Seller and Globe-Maker, 17 *n.*
Julien, Roch Joseph, 17, 27, 38, 41

Keere, Pieter van den, 15
Kip, William, 16
Kitchin, Thomas, 17
Krämer, Gerhard (1512–94) (see Mercator)

La Guillotière, François de, 26
Lamb, Francis, 45
Laplace, Pierre Simon, Marquis de (1749–1827), 47
La Rochelle, map of, 31
Lea, Philip, 15
Le Clerc, Jean, 7, 14, 26, 31
Le Clerc, veuve Jean, 14
Lhuyd, Humphrey (1527–68), 14
Lily, George, 15
Line of Demarcation, meridian of, 44
Lisle, Claude de (1644–1720), 17
Lisle, Guillaume de (1675–1726), 17
London, meridian of, 43, 44, 45

Manual of Map Reading and Field Sketching, 6, 50
Mediterranean, charts of, 10, 56
— coast-lines of, 37, 57
— dimensions of, 10, 12
Mercator, Gerhard (1512–94), 7, 8, 13, 14, 23, 37, 44
Miroir du Monde, Le, 13 *n.*, 14
Moll, Herman (d. 1732), 16, 44
Moore, Sir Jonas (1617–79), 19
Morden, Robert (d. 1704), 16
Morin, Jean Baptiste (1583–1656), 44
Mortier, Pierre, 35

Nangis, Guillaume de, 12
Naples, map of, 5, 27, 41
New Map of England and Wales, with part of Scotland, 45
Norden, John (1548–1625 or 6), 8, 15, 21

Ogilby, John (1600–76), 16
Old British mile, 16
Ordnance Survey, 18, 45, 50, 72, 73
Ortelius, Abraham (1527–98), 7, 8, 9, 13, 14, 23, 29, 37, 44, 55

Palestine, map of, 41
Paris, meridian of, 45
Picardy, cartographers of, 14
Picture of England, The, 42
Plantin, Christopher (1514–89), 7
Plantin Press, 7, 13*n.*
Portolan Charts, 8, 10, 12, 13, 22, 30, 36, 57, 59
Portolan Charts, their Origin and Characteristics, 12
Portuguese charts, 13
Posidonius (*c.* 130–50 B.C.), 10
Prospect of the Most Famous Parts of the World, 16
Ptolemy (Claudius Ptolemaeus) (*fl.* 127–151), 10, 11, 42, 44, 56, 57, 59

Reinels, the, 22
Reisecarte durch Deutschland (Etzlaub), 25
Richelieu, Cardinal de (1585–1642), 44
Rizzi-Zannoni, Giovanni Antonio, 5, 27, 41
Robert de Vaugondy, Gilles (1688–1766), 14, 17, 27
Robert de Vaugondy, Didier (1723–86), 14, 17, 27
Roy, Major-General William, 18
Ryther, Augustine (*fl.* 1576–90), 32, 32*n.*

Saint Michael, meridian of, 43, 44
Saint Paul's, meridian of, 45
Sanson, Adrien (d. 1708), 14
Sanson, Guillaume (d. 1703), 14
Sanson, Nicolas (1600–67), 4, 13, 14, 15, 26, 48, 49
Saxton, Christopher (*fl.* 1570–1610), 15, 21, 28*n.*, 32, 43
Seamen's Secrets, The, 43
Seller, John (*fl.* 1676–1700), 16, 45
Senex, John (d. 1740), 16
Sheldon, William (d. 1570), 21
Signot, Jacques, 25
Smith, William (1769–1839), 19, 33
Somer, Jean (*Pruthenus*), 26
Spanish Armada, charts of course of, 32
Speculum Britanniae, 8
Speculum Orbis Terrarum, 8
Speed, John (1555?–1629), 7, 16, 21, 28*n.*
Stevenson, Dr E. L., 12, 36
Studies in Carto-Bibliography, 4*n.*
Switzerland, maps of, 47, 48
Symeone, Gabriel, 31, 34

Tabula Peutingeriana, 11
Tapestry maps, monograph of, 21
Tassin, Nicolas, 23
Tavernier, Gabriel, 14
Tavernier, Melchior (1544–1641), 7, 14, 31, 32
Teesdales, the, 28
Teneriffe, meridian of, 44
Théâtre François, 7, 14, 37
Théâtre Géographique du Royaume de France (Le Clerc), 31
Théâtre Géographique du Royaume de France (Tavernier), 31
Theatre of the Empire of Great Britaine, 7, 16
Theatrum Orbis Terrarum, 7, 9, 13, 55
— Epitome of, 13*n.*
The 'Times' Atlas of the World, 33

Uzielli, 36

Vauban, Sebastien Le Prestre, Marquis de (1633–1707), 35
Visconte, Pietro, 12

Wells, Samuel, 19
Worrall, John, 15

Ziegler, 41